SUBMARINE
DEAD
AHEAD!

SUBMARINE
DEAD
AHEAD!

Waging Peace
in
America's Nuclear Colony

Kim Goldberg

HARBOUR PUBLISHING

Published by
HARBOUR PUBLISHING
P.O. Box 219
Madeira Park, BC Canada V0N 2H0

Edited by Laurel Bernard
Cover design by Roger Handling
Maps by Kelly Brooks

Canadian Cataloguing in Publication Data

Goldberg, Kim, 1954–
   Submarine dead ahead!

   Includes bibliographical references.
   ISBN 1-55017-053-8

   1. Nuclear submarines—British Columbia—Nanoose Bay—Testing.   2. Nuclear weapons—British Columbia—Nanoose Bay—Testing.   3. Antinuclear movement—British Columbia—Nanoose Bay.   4. Nuclear weapons—Government policy—Canada.   I. Title.
JX1974.7.G64 1991   327.1'74   C91-091563-6

CONTENTS

ACKNOWLEDGEMENTS

Writing may be a solitary pursuit, but those who support the writer can be legion. Five funding agencies saw fit to bankroll this project, thereby enabling me to pay the rent and keep guacamole on the table while I devoted myself to researching and writing the manuscript. My fiscal benefactors were the Canada Council, the Canadian Studies Directorate (Department of the Secretary of State), the Canadian Institute for International Peace and Security, the Franz Blumenfeld Peace Fund/Science for Peace, and Peacefund Canada. The views expressed in this book should not be taken to represent the views of any of the aforementioned funding agencies.

However, a writer does not live by money alone (although it's a pretty good start). I inflicted various portions of earlier drafts of this manuscript on the following resource people, each of whom obligingly read his or her sheaf of pages then politely set me straight on a thing or two and offered other useful suggestions: Norman Abbey, Robert Aldridge, Liberty Bradshaw, Maxine Carpenter, Deborah Ferens, Sunshine Goldstream, Tim Leadem, Laurie MacBride,

Donald Wells and Patricia Willis. Any mistakes that stubbornly persisted to the final draft are mine and mine alone.

To those who know me, it will come as no surprise that I plied, pestered and implored many other people for information, speculation and prognostication in the course of producing this book. My thanks to all who furnished me with data and ideas from within the peace movement, organized labour, the defence establishment, public office, communities affected by base closures, plus a few hard-to-categorize folks.

Without a publisher and editor, a writer has little more to show for her toil than a wad of paper and an eyestrain headache. Harbour Publishing kindly took this project beyond the wad stage. (Unfortunately, they couldn't do much about the headache.) And my editor Laurel Bernard had an uncanny ability for extracting a workable structure from a concatenation of facts and vignettes. She also wasn't too shabby at curbing my truly over-the-top stylistic moments (although, bird-lover that I am, I do miss my Nanoose rendition of Jonathan Livingston Seagull).

And finally, I owe much to the dedicated peace workers in the Nanoose Conversion Campaign, who inspired me with their vision and, on a more practical level, opened their burgeoning file drawers to me.

Kim Goldberg
Nanaimo, BC
October, 1991

INTRODUCTION

*No matter how much we may
accomplish here in Canada, I will
have failed in my most cherished
ambition if under my leadership
Canada has not helped reduce the
threat of war and enhanced the
promise of peace.*

Prime Minister Brian Mulroney
September 18, 1984

Six years and four months after Brian Mulroney revealed his most cherished ambition to the Canadian public, he plunged his country into war against a foreign nation for the first time in four decades. I had been living in Canada for nearly fourteen years when the Persian Gulf war began. My mother came up from Eugene, Oregon, in 1972 to get my younger brother out before he turned draft age and could be shipped to Vietnam. I stayed in Eugene long enough to finish my BA in Biology and then followed them up here to Nanaimo. We've been here ever since.

On January 16, 1991, when my mother phoned me and told me the war had begun, the first thing I felt was an immense heaviness, like I was sinking very quickly through the floor, through the con-

crete foundation of the building, through the bed-
rock beneath it, right down to the dark, dense core
of the earth. Then something inside me cracked
open, releasing a wave of sadness and hopelessness
like I have seldom known.

The force of my reaction shocked me. This war
was no surprise, after all. George Bush had spent
the entire fall amassing thousands of troops in some
faraway desert, steadfastly pre-empting all other
solutions to Saddam Hussein's invasion of Kuwait.
Mulroney waited a mere eight days after Saddam's
August 2 invasion before shipping Canadian troops
to the gulf. The world had even been given a dead-
line, a "countdown to war," as newscasters grimly
labelled it. Had I naïvely believed war would be
magically averted at the last minute?

Perhaps. But my sadness was more complex
than that, for I had just lost the last twenty years of
my life. It was 1971 again and I was reliving the US
government's zeal in pursuing a racist war against
dark-skinned people in a third world country. Vietnam one week, Iraq the next. The intervening years
had been erased for me, and along with them any
hope for breaking the pernicious pattern. Only this
time, it was worse. For there was no longer a neighbouring nation providing a real and symbolic haven
for war resistors. Canada was literally riding shot-
gun on America's bombing raids of Iraqi cities.

I asked myself why Canada—a country with a
proud reputation as a peacekeeper and as a shelter
for conscientious objectors—so readily fell into line
behind the US in this most recent immoral war. The
answer, or part of it, lurks just 15 kilometres from
my home on Vancouver Island. For in order to
understand Canada's growing subservience to the
US military apparatus at a time of war, I have dis-

covered one must understand Canada's integration, or more accurately absorption, into that apparatus during years of relative peace.

The Canadian Forces Maritime Experimental and Test Ranges (CFMETR) at Nanoose Bay, British Columbia, are among dozens of military staging grounds in Canada organically fused to the Pentagon's war-fighting strategies and nuclear infrastructure. For nearly three decades, the US Navy has tested and refined its anti-submarine warfare technology here—a technology essential for launching a pre-emptive first strike against the Soviet Union. Although the Nanoose operation should be a political relic from a now well-thawed Cold War, the US Navy's weapons-testing activities at Nanoose have not abated.

Prior to 1984, the US Navy's nuclear-powered, nuclear weapons-capable attack submarines quietly went about their deadly business in Nanoose Bay and Georgia Strait, generally unnoticed on the otherwise benign seascape. The Navy's invisibility came to an end one frosty November day when, under a cold, grey sky at the gates to CFMETR, the Nanoose Conversion Campaign was born. I was there covering the campaign's first Remembrance Day Nanoose peace walk. As a freelance reporter, I've continued to track the newsmaking, sub-chasing clutch of peaceful activists at Nanoose ever since. Editors at the Vancouver *Sun* and elsewhere were eager for the stories. The NCC's escapades made good copy: fifty people staging a "die-in" at the base gates, a pre-dawn skirmish between rubber lifeboats and Navy ships, protesters scrambling aboard nuclear subs, police arresting a human chain sealing off the entrance to the base, eight women rowing rickety dinghies through rough water to picnic on the shores of a military command centre, their trial five months later in a packed courtroom.

The months turned into years, and my work kept taking me back to the choppy waters at the mouth of the bay, to the gates of the base, to the peace camp of tipis (later the Peace House) across the bay, then home to my word processor and phone. The story didn't grow much beyond a few inches in the pages of any paper. But it grew before my eyes. The issues at Nanoose were broader, the implications of the Navy's work more sinister, the risks greater than I had first realized. And where I once saw caricatures of dishevelled protesters waging an impossible campaign against a monolithic force, I came to see dedicated peace workers living by their consciences and transcending the mass apathy, denial and inertia of a disempowered public. The group's ultimate goal of converting Nanoose to peaceful, productive uses—a goal which initially struck me as utopian—began to look not only plausible but inevitable.

My growing interest in the work and objectives of the peace movement took me abroad in 1987 to cover the anti-nuclear World Congress of Women in Moscow and the European Nuclear Disarmament Convention in Coventry, England. I had already decided to write this book. When I returned from Europe, and from the company of thousands of peace workers from scores of countries, I knew it was time to begin. I wanted to use the human-scale story of the Nanoose Conversion Campaign—the story I knew best—to address larger topics intersecting the Nanoose material. Topics such as first strike strategy, US maritime strategy, government policies affecting economic conversion of bases and industry, the nuclear-weapons-free zone movement, radiological risks posed by nuclear warships, and citizens' duties under international law. Topics that, without a personal and human component, would lie dead on the page, a meaningless stew of military expenditures, accident statistics, kill ratios and weapons specs.

After being exposed to the players and issues in the international peace movement, I began to realize that the Nanoose Conversion Campaign and the Nanoose base were each microcosms: the campaign, a microcosm of the hope, goals and vision of all people pursuing a nonviolent path in a violent world; and the base, a microcosm of a subordinate nation subsumed under the military agenda of a superpower.

Why look at these microcosms now? Because the Persian Gulf war was only the beginning—the beginning, George Bush assured us, of a new world order. However, all that's new about this order is its post-Cold War appearance. Even as a euphemism it belongs in a second-hand shop of newspeak. Fifty years earlier, a certain German chancellor promised the world a "great new order" marked by "a real understanding among peoples and . . . conciliation among nations." Adolph Hitler found the phrase so effective he titled his sequel to *Mein Kampf, My New Order*.

The intensity of my own reaction to the Gulf war and the anguish of being sucked through a memory hole back to the Vietnam years compelled me to sit down and whip this book into shape. For if there is to be a new world order, I would prefer to see it crafted by the likes of the Nanoose Conversion Campaign.

Chapter I

THE US NAVY AT HOME ON THE RANGE

In the town where we reside
There are certain things we like to hide
Yes, our harbour's very quaint
But at times it seems like what it ain't

Raging Grannies
(Tune: "Yellow Submarine")

I pulled into the rest stop alongside the bay, parked, shut off the lights, grabbed my mittens and camera bag, and headed toward the cluster of shadows and voices at the other end of the parking lot. A scent of brine and fir trees permeated the chill dark.

"Kim, hi! Glad you're here." It sounded like Miriam. A car streaked by on the highway, illuminating the group for a moment in an uneven flash of light. "We're just waiting for a couple of other media people to show up, and then we'll get started. Kevin's ferrying people out to the boat right now. If you go across the highway and get down to the shore, he'll pick you up on his next trip."

"Is there any coffee on the boat?" I asked groggily, unaccustomed to working (or being conscious) at 5:30 in the morning. It wasn't the most professional question. I should have been getting the facts. After all, that's what my editor was paying for. How many boats were they using? How many people? What did they intend to do? Did they plan to get arrested? Did the base know what was up?

"Yeah, Norm's got a pot on," Miriam answered. "And we'll give a press briefing on the boat."

This wasn't the first time I'd made the 15-kilometre drive up-island from my Nanaimo home to cover a protest against the US Navy's nuclear presence at Nanoose Bay in British Columbia. I'd been following the story for nearly two years, since November 1984, when a ragtag assortment of Vancouver Island peace activists launched the Nanoose Conversion Campaign in a bid to send the US Navy home and to convert the Navy's weapons-testing facility to peaceful uses. My interest in these people and their cause had grown steadily in the ensuing months, even if the inches editors allocated to my stories hadn't.

The cool September air slid past my cheeks as I shuffled over to the highway shoulder. Crossing the four-lane island highway at that spot is usually a daredevil feat more suited to Evel Knievel than a drowsy scribbler whose idea of risk is writing for twenty minutes without saving. Under normal circumstances, only the swiftest and boldest should attempt the death-defying sprint. But at that hour the dark swath of pavement was empty. I could have safely crawled across—a proposition that held certain sway within my foggy brain.

I headed straight for the coffee as soon as I boarded the *Gust O'*. The boat was already crowded. When I was downing my second cup, Richard from BCTV scrambled aboard with his video gear.

"OK. That's everybody," Miriam announced,

handing out press releases to the dim figures crammed into the cockpit and gangway of Norm's eleven-metre sloop. "Across the bay the USS *Bremerton* is sitting at dock." She pointed toward some shadowy, grey blobs along the far shore. "The *Bremerton* is a Los Angeles class, nuclear-powered and nuclear-capable attack submarine. We plan to go over there, board it and deliver a message to the captain."

"What? We're *all* going to board it?" Richard asked incredulously. Richard liked to get close to the action, but not quite that close.

"No, no," Miriam explained. "We'll stay here on the press boat. Just one or two people will board the sub. We have Greenpeace working with us today. The two Zodiacs are theirs. And the people who plan to board are from the Nanoose Conversion Campaign. The boat we're on now is . . ."

"Hey! They're heading out! Right now!" someone shouted from one of the Zodiacs in the water beside us.

"What? They're not supposed to leave for another two hours."

"It looks like they changed their plans. Someone must of tipped them."

"Let's go then!"

The Zodiacs sped out ahead in hot pursuit of the *Bremerton*, which was flanked by six military and RCMP patrol boats and a helicopter whirring overhead. By the time the chase reached the mouth of the bay and the open waters of Georgia Strait, the sky was filling up with light. The slow-moving *Gust O'* kept us well back of the action, which was not what the organizers had wanted. Good pictures were out of the question at this distance. My eyes would have to provide all the raw material for the story. I grabbed a pair of binoculars and watched the Zodiacs deftly maneuver among the throng of vessels out on the test range. One buzzed close enough to the sub for someone to shout: "We don't want nuclear weapons in Canadian waterways!" But there was no response and no hope of boarding at that speed, so the Zodiacs turned back.

Defeated but not beaten, the disarmers returned to the highway rest stop to plot their next strategy. The sub had to come in from the range sooner or later.

When the massive *Bremerton*, displacing 6,000 tons of ocean, finally headed in after a full day of anti-submarine warfare trials, it quickly found itself stalled in the calm waters of Nanoose Bay by 150 metres of polypropylene rope and bobbing bleach bottles laid down by a haphazard assortment of boats and dinghies.

What next?

Ted Phillips, a fifty-one-year-old grandfather and twenty-year veteran of the British Royal Navy, didn't stop to ask that question. He just stripped down to his underwear, dove into the icy water, stroked quickly over to the *Bremerton*, tried unsuccessfully to gain a purchase on the sub's sloping hull, settled instead for the adjacent tugboat, grabbed hold of a large cleat and began hauling himself up. The RCMP Zodiac made a few confused lurches to the left and right before fighting its way through the chaotic frenzy of boats, dinghies, military vessels, floating rope, Purex jugs and a captive sub, whereupon Ted was promptly intercepted and dragged into the police Zodiac.

"I didn't really notice the temperature of the water with all that bedlam going on," Ted told me by phone that night when he returned home from the Parksville lock-up. "I wanted to reach the sub and ask the captain whether he was carrying nuclear weapons on board and what kind of safeguards he had in case of a nuclear reactor accident."

It was ironic, I thought, that someone who had served two decades in Britain's nuclear navy was now risking hypothermia and a jail sentence to protest America's nuclear navy. As though reading my thoughts, Ted explained the paradox.

"After twenty years in the military in which I thought I was defending England against the Nazis, now I ask myself: What can I do to defend my six grandchildren against this nuclear thing?"

However, the question resounding in my head at that moment was: What is this nuclear thing doing in Nanoose Bay?

I. Nintendo Anyone?

Beneath the wailing gulls and undulating waters of Georgia Strait near Nanoose Bay on the east coast of Vancouver Island, an electronic web of listening devices lies anchored to 130 square kilometres of muddy seabed. A short distance away, on a jagged pile of rocks called North Winchelsea Island, a handful of men hover around video monitors inside a glass-walled command centre and eyeball the computerized display of objects slicing through the sea above the hydrophones. The results of these trials tell the US Navy how fast and accurate its anti-submarine warfare (ASW) weapons are, what can fool them and what needs to be fixed to make them better, faster and smarter.

In 1986, I hitched a ride out to North Winchelsea Island aboard a military patrol boat to check out the set-up for myself. As soon as I stepped through the door, base officials told me to keep my camera capped and in my bag. Too bad, I thought. George Lucas would pay dearly to glimpse this prototype for a new *Star Wars* set—a few extraterrestrial console operators and, presto, *Episode Four: The Empire Comes Back for More.*

In the centre of the room a bank of video screens mounted in a long, curved console flash computer-generated colour graphics tracing the three-dimensional path and position of the weapon, target, target vessel, firing craft and support vessels on the range. To one side of the elaborate video display, enormous picture windows frame the sweeping panorama of the inky strait dotted with greyish naval vessels. On the other side of the console, refrigerator-sized mainframe computers purr quietly. The test data, which include the torpedo's speed, search pattern and success of attack, are stored on magnetic tape and plotter printouts for later analysis.

This is called the Canadian Forces Maritime Experimental and Test Ranges. In total, it occupies approximately 500 square kilometres of Canadian land and water at Nanoose Bay and Georgia Strait in coastal British Columbia. The semi-rural environs of Nanoose support a population of 3,700. The 50,000 residents of Nanaimo are a 15-kilometre drive south on the island. The bay itself is shared by boaters, paddlers, commercial oyster beds, and a fish farm, while the Nanoose Indian Band sits on a stretch of bay shoreline opposite the naval docks.

The military site is commonly referred to as the Nanoose test range or simply the Nanoose base, although technically it's not a base but a field unit of Canada's Department of National Defence. The DND usually refers to the installation by its official acronym: CFMETR (pronounced "See Eff Meter").

The facilities and testing areas at Nanoose include a main dock and storage building at Ranch Point on Nanoose Bay, a smaller dock and administrative headquarters also on Nanoose Bay, the command centre on North Winchelsea Island in Georgia Strait, and three torpedo test ranges in the strait. (See maps, pages 154-156.) Only one of the three ranges, WG or "Whiskey Golf," is fully instrumented for remote monitoring of the three-dimensional path of a mobile underwater object. For that reason, it's the most heavily used. Fifty-five kilometres up the strait a fourth test range lies in Jervis Inlet with a sonobuoy test site nearby in Hotham Sound.

The US Navy uses CFMETR primarily to test the guidance systems on its non-nuclear acoustic homing torpedoes and ASROCs (Anti-submarine Rockets) and to develop sonobuoys. But the US Navy can from time to time find other good uses for friendly Canadian waters: the USS *Nimitz*, one of the world's largest warships, has turned up at Nanoose more than once for sea trials. Canada also conducts ASW research at Nanoose in the form of torpedo, ASROC and sonobuoy testing as well as hydrophone repair. Canadian ASW trials account for 10–25 percent of the range time annually, with the rest going to the US.

II. Remote Control

The Canadian government is quick to deny the charge that Nanoose is merely a branch plant for American war planning. "CFMETR is a Canadian facility... There is no United States commander involved," the Prime Minister's office assured the Vancouver Island Network for Disarmament in 1982. Indeed, according to a 1965 agreement signed by both countries, the test ranges are jointly operated by the United States and Canada, and the agreement states: "the facility shall be a Canadian Forces station, and the Canadian Armed Forces shall be responsible for administration, security and operational control."

But while the day-to-day administration of the overall base may nominally rest in Canadian hands, the scheduling of the ASW trials on the instrumented range—by far the most significant activity at Nanoose— is another story. A US Navy instruction manual issued by the United States Pacific Fleet headquartered in Pearl Harbor states the "scheduling authority. . . and the conduct of range operations [for the Nanoose Underwater Tracking Range] are under the cognizance and responsibility of the Commanding Officer, Naval Torpedo Station (NTS), Keyport, Washington." Located 200 kilometres southeast of Nanoose, Keyport is the nerve centre for the Naval Undersea Warfare Engineering Station (NUWES). And when the US Navy is running ASW tests at Nanoose, a US Navy range officer is calling the shots on-site.

In a NUWES information brochure, the Navy grants Nanoose a "US/Canadian" status but identifies the site as part of the NUWES complex, whose role is to service American naval needs. In describing NUWES, the US Navy boasts: "A complete modern light industrial complex supports undersea weapon test and evaluation in the Pacific Northwest and on nearby US/Canadian Ranges. . . NUWES has the assigned mission, organization, facilities and expertise to initiate advancements in undersea weapons, to develop, test and evaluate them, and to integrate them into the operating Navy."

In addition to scheduling the ASW trials at Nanoose, the US Navy owns the $100 million of computers and underwater monitoring equipment that track the weapons out on the range and then record and compile the data at the command centre. Canada owns the building in which the computers are housed and the razor-wire fence surrounding it. Although the base is staffed by a greater number of Canadians than Americans (108 as opposed to 67), the bulk of the Canadian staff are civilian. The majority of military staff at CFMETR are American.

Historically, the US and Canadian navies have each been faced with the problem of finding suitable waters in which they could run their torpedoes and test them to their design limits. Prior to 1966, the US Navy tested its torpedoes at Dabob Bay and Hood Canal, both near Keyport. Canada meanwhile was running its own torpedo test range at Patricia Bay near Victoria on the south end of Vancouver Island. But technology does not stand still. Torpedoes were getting faster, "smarter" and more versatile. They eventually outgrew the confined waters of these ranges, as the DND explains in its hand-out on CFMETR:

"As torpedoes became more sophisticated, their speeds increased, acquisition ranges increased, operating depths were extended, and run times increased. . . An area in the Strait of Georgia adjacent to Nanoose Harbour seemed ideally suited for such activities. The area was of interest to the USN as it met most of their additional requirements for the operation of a fully-instrumented 3-D tracking range."

The Nanoose site was evaluated in 1962, and the US Navy deemed the spot suitable for its needs. Three years later, an official diplomatic agreement was drawn up and signed by the two countries detailing the terms for the "establishment, operation and maintenance of a torpedo test range in the Strait of Georgia." In 1966, the range became operational. The joint agreement has subsequently been renewed at ten-year intervals in 1976 and 1986, respectively, and is next due for renewal in 1996.

Although it may be situated in Canada, the Nanoose underwater weapons testing range has little significance to Canadian national security and defence planning. "The importance of the Nanoose range to Canada is negligible," former US Army intelligence analyst William Arkin told me and a couple of other reporters gathered at Nanoose one afternoon for a press conference. "It's important to the United States . . . The range doesn't exist for the Canadian Navy to be able to test its torpedoes and sonobuoys. The range exists for the United States forces on the west coast to do that," said Arkin, who currently heads up the Nuclear Information Unit at Greenpeace USA in Washington, DC.

III. A Whale of a Problem

Base officials insist they recover every spent torpedo from the ASW trials at Nanoose. But during informal conversations on CFMETR's periodic open house days, I've heard at least one base worker say they occasionally "lose" one. In 1986, four sport fishermen spotted a Mark-46 near Galiano Island, 43 kilometres south of the test range. A week earlier, CFMETR had broadcast a warning to boaters in the strait cautioning them to be on the lookout for a stray torpedo and not to touch it if they saw it.

Recovering the sub sinkers can be a headache, and a costly one with each Mark-48 ringing in at $1 million. According to a DND document released through the Access to Information Act, the US Navy retrieved approximately 1,600 "units" (i.e., spent torpedoes) between 1971 and 1981 at CFMETR.

The Navy thought it had the retrieval problem licked in 1981 when it drafted a couple of good-natured belugas, whale-napped four years earlier from Hudson Bay. After undergoing eight months of basic training at NUWES headquarters, the whales were deployed to Nanoose. Newspaper editors had some fun with "Beluga Whale, Navy Recruit," but conservationists were furious. "It's a perversion," said Bob Nixon of the Sierra Club in Victoria. "It's training life to obliterate life." Greenpeace Canada's communications director was equally unhappy. "It's disgusting that a species that has lived in peace for millions of years is to be used to take part in military exercises," Bob Cummings remarked.

Greenpeace even slipped in one night and liberated the aquatic conscripts from their sea pens. One local angler's heart skipped a beat when the female beluga popped up in the middle of an RCMP fishing derby. The Navy was relieved to find her, since she'd been given up for lost, and the Nanaimo alderman who almost reeled her in went home with fourth prize for a five-and-a-half-pound coho. According to base officials, both whales voluntarily returned to their military duties and to their guaranteed daily ration of 18 kilos of fish apiece.

Despite the belugas' loyalty, the Navy ultimately gave them their discharge papers, officially because they weren't altogether effective at their job. When I asked one old-time base employee why the Navy sent the whales packing, he said it was because "they ate too much."

IV. Nukes R Us

From 1984 through 1990, nuclear-capable warships (i.e., submarines or surface ships that are fitted and

certified to carry nuclear weapons), spent 253 ship-
days at Nanoose, according to DND records obtained
by Project Ploughshares and Operation Dismantle
through the Access to Information Act. The question
of whether nuclear warheads are actually aboard the
warships when they come to non-nuclear Canada is
clumsily and tediously skirted by Washington and
Ottawa.

"It is the policy of allied nuclear powers own-
ing nuclear-capable vessels neither to confirm nor
deny the presence of nuclear weapons on board the
vessels. It is the policy of the Canadian government
to respect this policy," J.B. Peart, chief of staff for the
Canadian defence minister's office told the Nanoose
Conversion Campaign.

But while Washington is neither confirming
nor denying, there is little doubt among experienced naval officers as to the status of nuclear-capable warships. A US Navy veteran of thirty-five
years, retired Admiral Eugene Carroll maintains: "It
has been my experience that all US warships that
are capable of carrying nuclear weapons do carry
nuclear weapons . . . To be combat ready and meet
all our missions, they have to be nuclear equipped."

However, it seems the war business ain't what
it used to be. Due to declining superpower tensions
(and budgets) plus technical obsolescence, the US
Navy began a process of "spontaneous disarmament"
and denuclearization in 1989, phasing out its ASROC,
SUBROC and Terrier nuclear weapon systems. Con-
sequently, some of the Navy's ships and subs plying
Nanoose Bay and Georgia Strait today are no longer
nuclear-capable.

Nevertheless, a number of the Navy's warships
visiting Nanoose continue to be nuclear-capable as
well as nuclear-powered. In 1990, seven nuclear-

capable warships (six of which were also nuclear-powered), spent a total of nineteen ship-days at Nanoose. In the first nine months of 1991, warship visits at Nanoose had climbed up to thirty-one ship-days logged by seven nuclear-capable and nuclear-powered vessels. And, although the warships don't test their nuclear weapons at Nanoose, the US Navy's floating nuclear arsenals and nuclear reactors bobbing around in the bay are a radiological time bomb.

Chapter 2

DEADLY GEOMETRY: BC'S NUCLEAR TRIANGLE

*When there are nuclear weapons,
there are going to be accidents.*

External Affairs Minister Joe Clark
House of Commons, June 8, 1989

I wouldn't have believed it if I hadn't read it with my own eyes, but the Soviet tour company, Kievturist, figures there's a market for meltdowns. Hence, the company's hottest package tour: Radioactive Sites of the Ukraine.

According to a February 1991 report in *Komsomolskaya Pravda* newspaper, those who dare can roam the pulsating environs of Chernobyl, scope out a radioactive waste dump at Kopachi, meditate on the concrete sarcophagus entombing reactor No. 4 that blew in 1986 and amble through Slavutich—home to thousands of workers who still crank out the kilowatts at Chernobyl's three remaining reactors. Kievturist even throws in a Geiger counter test at the beginning and end of the jaunt. And if anyone needs to be hauled away and scrubbed down at a radiological medical centre, the company says it will pick up the tab (for the treatment, not the tour).

I. Canada's Own Bermuda Triangle

Appalling as this experiment in free enterprise sounds, a similar tourist draw may be all that's left for "super-natural" British Columbia if one of the US Navy's nuclear-powered ships or submarines suffers a reactor core meltdown while visiting BC. It's little wonder the Nanoose Conversion Campaign refers to the nuclear subs at Nanoose as "floating Chernobyls." And Nanoose Bay isn't the Navy's only nuclear hitching post in this province. The sleepy, fir-draped, semi-rural community shares that privilege with Victoria's CFB Esquimalt on the southern tip of Vancouver Island and with the major urban centre of Vancouver on the mainland across Georgia Strait.

Nuclear-capable warships turn up at all three ports throughout the year, while nuclear-powered vessels are restricted to Nanoose and Esquimalt. In 1989, Esquimalt had the dubious honour of being Canada's busiest nuclear port, while Vancouver drew third place and Nanoose fourth. (Halifax ranked second.) From 1980 through 1990, 114 nuclear-capable warships spent a total of 1,417 ship-days in BC's nuclear triangle, according to DND records obtained by Project Ploughshares and Operation Dismantle through the Access to Information Act. That's one nuclear-capable warship every three days. The frequency soared to nearly one warship per day in 1986 when Vancouver hosted Expo '86, a transportation and communications world fair.

While the Navy's reason for putting in at Nanoose is connected to the ASW program, the other two corners of BC's nuclear triangle can attribute their popularity primarily to the Navy's desire to keep its warships on the move, to grab a little R and

R for the crew, and to show the flag and maintain a visible presence in "friendly" nations. The total human population encompassed by BC's nuclear triangle approaches two million. The waters, which yield up a bounty of fish and shellfish, are criss-crossed with ferry routes linking Vancouver Island to the mainland and the gulf islands. Commercial fish boats, pleasure craft, freighters, tugs, log tows, railway barges and cruise ships ply the strait, inlets and bays day and night, year round. And weaving among them are the US Navy's nuclear-powered and nuclear-capable subs and surface ships.

II. A Tomb With a View

Friendship is great. But what do you do when near-ly half (56) of the 114 nuclear-capable warships your friend brings over for dinner have messy acci-dent histories? Those, unfortunately, are the stats for the nuclear warships turning up in BC waters, according to the list of naval accidents documented in *Neptune Papers* #3 and #4 by William Arkin and Joshua Handler of Greenpeace USA. Nanoose is also batting 50 percent. Of the 47 nuclear-capable war-ships dropping anchor at Nanoose between 1980 and 1990 (inclusive), 24 brought a dismal accident record with them. The accident toll of BC's nuclear visitors includes numerous deaths (both crew and civilian), radiation contamination plus damage to naval and civilian vessels both at sea and at port, the world over—and all during non-combat activity.

It's little wonder that Greenpeace, Greater Victo-ria Disarmament Group, Nanoose Conversion Cam-paign, Raging Grannies and other anti-nuclear groups within BC's nuclear triangle have for years been waging peace against the nuclear mammoths in their harbours with relentless, if outmatched, determination. Among their many tactics, protesters have chained themselves to warships and piers, conducted a swim-in around a warship and a sing-in at a base, boarded a sub, chased a sub around a harbour, and scaled the cables of a suspension bridge to a height 100 metres above the water to unfurl a huge banner proclaiming "Nuclear Free Seas."

All nuclear reactors and nuclear weapons pose potential radiological risks to the surrounding population and environment. Naval nuclear reactors offer the unenviable prospect of low-level radiation contamination from a leaky reactor or accidental spill discharging radioactive effluent into the water. At least five of the Navy's nuclear-powered ships and subs touring BC's nuclear triangle in the 1980s brought with them an ominous history of reactor leaks.

These same reactors could be a source of high-level radiation contamination in the event of a fire (an alarmingly common occurrence on docked ships) or a reactor core meltdown. A shipboard fire could potentially leave portions of coastal BC radioactive and uninhabitable for years if the blaze reached any of the nuclear warheads these vessels are certified to carry. Other accident scenarios involving nuclear weapons include sabotage, dropping a weapon overboard or unintentional firing.

This grim reality has been nagging at least a few people in BC's radiant triangle for several years. In 1987, the Victoria chapter of the Canadian Physicians for the Prevention of Nuclear War, along with the Greater Victoria Disarmament Group, Greenpeace and Operation Dismantle, decided to find out how bad the bad news was. They commissioned a study evaluating the potential effects of a naval nuclear accident in Victoria/Esquimalt, an area with nearly 300,000 inhabitants.

In his 139-page report, Dr. Jackson Davis of the University of Santa Cruz concluded that if a nuclear weapon accident occurred aboard one of the US warships at CFB Esquimalt, "medically and environmentally significant doses of radiation would be expected up to 100 kilometres from the accident site." Depending on wind conditions, more than one million people could be affected because "the effects of such an accident could be experienced as far away as Vancouver."

The scenario involving a reactor accident would be slightly less catastrophic, Davis says. However, both accident scenarios "would cause from hundreds to thousands of long-term casualties unless the contaminated urban areas were both evacuated and decontaminated. Rapid evacuation would appear impossible in the absence of effective emergency response plans." Not only would some or all of Greater Victoria have to be evacuated within a couple of hours, the procedures for decontaminating a large urban area have yet to be pioneered. Without complete decontamination—a task the US government prices in the tens of billions of dollars—BC's provincial capital would be aglow for decades or even millennia, depending on the type of accident. The cesium-137 that would be released in a reactor accident has a half-life of 30 years. The plutonium-239 from a nuclear weapon accident has a half-life of 24,500 years.

Pondering the prospect of being vaporized or slowly irradiated is not a new pastime for coastal British Columbians. Back in 1973, residents were wrinkling their foreheads when an official from CFB Esquimalt blithely told a Victoria newspaper:

"It's not uncommon for an American nuclear submarine to put into base [at Nanoose]. About once a
month one will arrive to be monitored for radiation." Ironically, when Major Vic Keating made the
remark, he was trying quell public objections to
CFMETR following an anti-Vietnam war protest.
But his admission had the reverse effect by opening
up a previously unconsidered dimension to the US
Navy's presence at Nanoose Bay.

Later, Keating tried to back-pedal. He told reporters uninformed residents were spreading the
ugly rumour that the Navy was using Nanoose to
test its subs for reactor leaks. He conceded that all
nuclear submarines coming into Nanoose were monitored for radiation, but emphasized "There has
never been a leak to date to our knowledge either
in Canadian or US waters. In other words, nuclear
submarines do not leak."

III. Here's Leaking at You, Kid

Around the same time the Major was singing the
safety record of nuclear subs, the USS *Guardfish* (an
attack sub that has shown its conning tower at both
Nanoose and Esquimalt) was leaking primary coolant while running submerged off northwestern US.
Four sailors were subsequently transferred to Puget
Sound Naval Hospital for radiation monitoring. Keating's ignorance can perhaps be forgiven since it
took another decade before public interest groups
could wring any accident disclosures out of the US
Navy. The same, however, cannot be said for the
countless government and military officials on both
sides of the border who have followed in his ora-
tory footsteps.

"In the past 20 years that such visits around the

world including Canada have occurred, they have taken place without injury to the public or the environment as the result of nuclear propulsion or nuclear weapons incident," the Mulroney government wrote in a July 1988 position paper titled "Canada and Nuclear Weapons." In fact, as late as April 1991, a few days before he was sent off to tend the agriculture portfolio, Defence Minister Bill McKnight informed the Greater Victoria Disarmament Group that "there has been no known accidental release of radioactive materials in over twenty-five years of operations by allied nuclear-propelled vessels. I think you will agree with me that this is an impressive safety record."

But in 1983, the Fund for a Constitutional Government and the Center for Investigative Reporting (two US organizations) revealed that since 1954 there had been at least 126 accidents involving the world's nuclear navies. At least 54 directly involved a vessel's nuclear reactor—many aboard US Navy submarines and many causing radioactive contamination.

Together with the Neptune papers released in 1989 and 1990, this mountain of research showed that, for decades, nuclear submarines had been running aground, sinking, catching fire, getting tangled in fishnets or lost at sea, experiencing "minor" leaks and accidental spills of radioactive coolant, and colliding with harbour tugs, fish boats and enemy subs all over the globe. The consequences of these documented accidents included hundreds of crew deaths, numerous crew members exposed to radiation, and thousands of gallons of reactor coolant leaked, spilled or in some cases purposely dumped into rivers, harbours and oceans. In particular, the Navy's attack submarines *Guardfish*, *Gurnard* and

Hawkbill, the guided-missile cruiser *California* and the gargantuan *Nimitz* aircraft carrier can't seem to stay out of trouble—leaky or otherwise. So far these BC visitors have managed to have their accidents elsewhere.

In addition to its 1973 leak, the *Guardfish* has run aground twice, once coming to rest neatly atop a sand-filled practice bomb on a reef in Pearl Harbor. In 1980, 30 gallons of radioactive water sloshed into San Diego Bay when a sailor aboard the *Gurnard* accidentally opened the wrong valve. Nine years later (and just three months after the sub stopped over at Nanoose) the *Gurnard*'s captain was relieved of his command in May 1989 after running the sub aground during a routine training exercise near San Diego.

The *Hawkbill*, which, like the *Guardfish*, jockeys between Esquimalt and Nanoose taking in the sights of 100 kilometres of Georgia Strait along the way, first sprung a leak in 1979. It lost two gallons of reactor coolant per hour for four days while on maneuvers in Hawaiian waters and later while ported at Pearl Harbor. The radiation was reportedly contained on board. The Navy shrugged and said "such leaks happen occasionally," which proved doubly true in the *Hawkbill*'s case. Next year, the *Hawkbill* leaked at least 150 gallons of reactor coolant while sitting in the Puget Sound Naval Shipyard in Bremerton, Washington. This time five workers were contaminated—two internally. In each case, a faulty valve was the culprit.

Moving on to surface ships, the *California*, which spends time at Esquimalt, has twice spilled primary reactor coolant while docked at the Norfolk Naval Base in Virginia. And the *Nimitz*, powered by two nuclear reactors, has the most dismal record of all. So bad, in fact, that in August 1990, four sailors walked off the deck and into a Seattle TV station. With their faces and voices electronically altered during the broadcast to protect their identities, the sailors told of widespread cheating on nuclear qualification tests, faulty hardware, overworked crews and reactor problems. In the event of a reactor accident "we could not contain the radiation," one sailor stated. Some of the crew, they said, were so concerned about the safety of the vessel and those aboard that they were contemplating sabotage to keep the *Nimitz* safely docked at Bremerton.

The Navy quickly rounded up the four whistleblowers (no doubt with stern admonitions about loose lips sinking ships), hustled them back aboard the aircraft carrier and promptly headed out on a thirty-day training cruise with Georgia Strait and Nanoose at the top of the itinerary. It's unclear how much hardware the *Nimitz* was packing when it motored into BC and up the Strait. However, when fully decked out, this leviathan warship hauls about 80 nuclear-capable aircraft and a crew of 6,000.

The record—or at least the official version—tells us the *Nimitz* suffered its first and only reactor leak of primary coolant back in 1979 somewhere off the Virginia coastline. However, the carrier's accident woes didn't end there. Two years later, fourteen crew were killed and forty-eight injured when a blaze broke out after an aircraft crashed onto the *Nimitz* while trying to land. The ship was operating about 100 kilometres off Jacksonville, Florida, at the time. In 1988, while touring the Arabian Sea, a cannon aboard one of the carrier's aircraft "accidentally discharged" (in naval parlance), torching six other aircraft on deck and killing one crew member. The fact that cracks were discovered in January 1990 in the primary coolant circuits of the British counterpart to the *Nimitz*'s aging Westinghouse reactors has not eased crew anxiety.

In August 1991, inhabitants of BC's nuclear triangle were given a preview of the type of naval disaster looming in their waters when a US Navy attack submarine ripped into the net of a commercial fish boat near the mouth of the Fraser River. Fortunately for the fisherman and his fifteen-year-old grandson on board, the USS *Omaha* (a nuclear-powered attack sub fitted to carry Tomahawk cruise missiles) was able to free itself without disaster. Mirko Tolja went home without his net that day. But at least he went home.

Tolja's near-miss with the nuclear-capable sub raises some interesting questions, one of which is: would we necessarily know if radioactive contamination resulted from a warship accident? The US Department of Defense directive 5230.16 conveniently permits the US Navy or other government representatives to deny or conceal a nuclear weapon accident: "Unified Commanders . . . may confirm or deny the presence of nuclear weapons or radioactive nuclear weapon components at the scene of an accident or significant incident in the interests of public safety or to reduce public alarm."

Nevertheless, in 1986, after a five-year legal battle with the Pentagon, the American Friends Service Committee released government documents obtained through the Freedom of Information Act summarizing twelve years of naval nuclear weapon accidents categorized by the US Navy as "broken arrows," "bent spears" or "dull swords" depending on their severity. Between 1965 and 1977 the

US Navy incurred 381 accidents or "incidents" with its nuclear weapons including several instances of "inadvertent release"—an event soberly defined by the Navy as "a launch or firing other than planned."

The most comprehensive revelation of accidents involving nuclear-powered vessels and nuclear weapons appeared in 1989 with the *Neptune Papers #3*—an extensive report on naval accidents spanning 1945 to 1988 jointly published by the Washington-based Institute for Policy Studies and Greenpeace USA. *Neptune Papers #3* details 1,276 accidents, including 212 involving nuclear-powered subs and warships, racked up by the world's major navies during the forty-three-year period.

Even these figures proved to be just the tip of a radioactive iceberg. In 1990, the authors revised their survey after digging up additional primary source material including computer printouts from the US Navy's Naval Safety Center. In the last decade alone (1980–1989), US nuclear-powered attack submarines, including several visitors to BC's nuclear triangle, logged 451 accidents around the planet. The numbers climb higher still when the fender benders, spills and screw-ups of other nuclear navies are figured in. No less than 3,200 naval accidents—almost one per day— were brought to us in the 1980s, courtesy of the world's five nuclear navies. Worldwide warship casualties accruing from accidents (excluding war or military conflict) include fifty nuclear warheads and eight nuclear reactors lying somewhere on the ocean floor plus more than 2,800 direct deaths.

IV. Inert NERTs

The Nanoose Conversion Campaign argues that the floating nuclear reactors touring BC waters at the whim of the US Navy have escaped all public input procedures and environmental impact studies any commercial nuclear power plant would be subjected to. Not only are naval nuclear reactors shielded from public scrutiny, they pose additional risks beyond the already serious risks attached to commercial, land-based reactors. They are aboard moving vessels involved in various activities, increasing the chance of fire or collision. They possess proportionally smaller containment devices because of shipboard space limitations. They are fueled by uranium that's thirty times more enriched than commercial fuel, making it weapons-grade material. And they operate closer to their maximum thermal limits than commercial, land-based reactors do (once again because of shipboard space limitations), thereby increasing the likelihood of fuel damage and meltdown.

Compounding the hazards, if a nuclear reactor aboard a US warship at Nanoose ran afoul, the ailing vessel would have to limp or be towed out to sea—a journey that would take many hours and pass most major population centres on Vancouver Island along the way.

Even the federal government acknowledges that a naval nuclear reactor accident is a possible consequence of a port call. Ottawa stringently bars nuclear-powered vessels from all civilian ports and only allows the Navy's floating nuclear reactors to enter Canada's three military ports: Esquimalt, Nanoose and Halifax. Nuclear-capable but conventionally powered vessels, on the other hand, can tie up anywhere the water's deep enough as far as Ottawa is concerned, including major, non-military, commercial ports such as Vancouver. The reason Ottawa keeps nuclear-powered warships on a shorter tether is because of the different risk factor, the External Affairs office says.

"The threat posed by nuclear weapons in such circumstances—in the event such weapons actually were carried by these ships—would be minimal," John Fowell, director of defence relations, assured me. "There is no danger, for example, of these weapons leaking radioactivity. There is, on the other hand, a theoretical possibility of such leaks occurring from a nuclear propulsion system. It is for this reason that nuclear-powered vessels are prohibited from all but certain designated ports where Nuclear Emergency Response Teams (NERTs) are located to contain damage that might result from a nuclear accident or leak."

Ah yes, the mythic NERTs—those white-suited men from Glad who will swoosh in, sop up any unsightly radiation, and leave our nautical environs sparkling in the late afternoon sun. Of course, the fact that Nanoose has no NERT within 100 kilometres seems to have escaped Ottawa's attention. Vancouver is also NERTless, due to the government's insistence that only nuclear reactors, not nuclear weapons, pose a risk in Canadian ports. Victoria, the seat of BC's provincial government, fares somewhat better, having a resident NERT at CFB Esquimalt. However, a nearby NERT may provide nothing more than a false sense of security.

The DND's response plan for a nuclear emergency at military sites is classified, but some limited information has leaked out. In the event of a nuclear accident, a NERT will show up, cordon off and evacuate an area with a radius of 609 metres in the case of a nuclear weapon accident or 550 metres for a naval propulsion reactor accident. There is no evidence that DND or any other government agency has developed a plan to respond to the specific circumstances of an emergency involving nuclear contamination beyond this radius.

The NERTs aren't the only precaution Ottawa claims to be employing to protect the public from a radiological catastrophe at nuclear ports. Water and sediment samples are routinely scooped up around the dock before, during and after a visit from a nuclear-powered vessel, then analyzed at the Radiation Protection Services lab in Vancouver. But apparently no one has turned the scope on the resident shellfish, who spend their entire lives sitting in the mud merrily filtering and accumulating whatever comes their way. In fact, the federal government seems to be downright confused about whether the shellfish and fin fish commercially farmed beneath the nuclear subs at Nanoose Bay could be bringing a radiant glow to someone's supper table.

"At no time have radioactive materials ever been found [at Nanoose Bay or Esquimalt] despite rigorous adherence to prescribed monitoring protocols," the Canadian Forces Fleet School in Esquimalt told a concerned Powell River resident in June 1990. The military's missive left Martin Rossander perplexed since two months earlier Environment Canada had given him this response: "Primary sources of radioactive materials in shellfish-growing areas are visiting nuclear submarines from the United States and Britain. The areas most susceptible to radioactive contamination on the west coast from this source are Nanoose Bay, Esquimalt Harbour and Victoria Harbour . . . Radioactive compounds detected at these locations are Iodine, Cobalt and Cesium, however, the levels have always been very low . . . Some shellfish do selectively accumulate radionuclides in their shells or soft tissues."

Not surprisingly, peace groups and even some local governments within BC's nuclear zone want to know who's handling the emergency response plan for protecting, evacuating and treating civilians in the event of a naval nuclear accident. However, it does not appear that either federal, provincial or local governments have devised (or even given much thought to) any sort of plausible emergency response plan to cope with the civilian population during and after a nuclear catastrophe. Coastal BC's earthquake preparedness plan won't be much use against a radioactive plume leaving scores of people too hot to handle and certainly too hot to pile into ambulances or emergency hospitals without contaminating all vehicles, equipment and health care workers.

Since 1986, the Nanoose Conversion Campaign has been demanding public disclosure and discussion of DND's emergency response plan for CFMETR. Not that DND's plan would do much for civilians. But at least civilian planners could start to develop a co-ordinated strategy. In late 1989, DND finally responded (in a way) after Parksville municipal council echoed the NCC's call for disclosure of the emergency plan. (Parksville, a town of 6,000, lies 10 kilometres north of Nanoose.)

DND invited the whole gang over to CFMETR for the world premier of the base's flashy, new, $50,000 promotional video (imaginatively titled "CFMETR") and a casual après-flick chat with base Commander Dan McVicar. About fifteen members of the NCC showed up along with Parksville's emergency program co-ordinator and myself. After viewing DND's travelogue, the mythic emergency plan was the first question on most people's lips. Commander McVicar dispatched a few routine queries about radiation monitoring and torpedo models, only to be continually pestered by: "Yeah but, what do we do if. . . " Surprised by the persistent interest in this topic, the young and personable commander decided it was time to set everyone's mind at ease.

"I think it's well known what to do in the case of a radiation leak," he tossed off casually. The up-to-now subdued and courteous audience erupted with boisterous shouts and cries.

"What?"

"No, we *don't* know!"

"Tell us!"

The startled commander, himself a father of three young girls, replied in his customarily open and affable style: "You get away from it, of course," obviously wondering how anyone could be so dense as to not know this elementary fact of life. The audience gaped in silence at McVicar, stunned by his "These Boots are Made for Walking" emergency response plan.

At the end of the confab, McVicar did assure the group that DND would be releasing details of CFMETR's emergency plan to civilian emergency planners in the new year. As of September 1991, twenty-one months after the promise, no such disclosure had occurred.

Chapter 3

NUCLEAR FREE:
TO BE OR NOT TO BE

*Canada does not have nuclear
weapons on its soil, nor shall it
during the life of this government.*

Prime Minister Brian Mulroney
March 1985

When Canada's PM of six months pledged to
keep his country's dirt nuclear free, he must
have crossed his fingers and hoped nobody listening would question him on the distinction between
dirt and water. For although Canada may not have
nuclear weapons on its soil, it certainly has them in
its ports and waterways—and regularly.

For an increasing number of Canadians, the
federal government's practice of disallowing nuclear weapons on Canadian soil while regularly
allowing them in Canadian water constitutes a serious breach of national sovereignty. "If a foreign
nation can station major nuclear weapons in the
heart of some of our cities, making them targets in
any nuclear exchange, without officially informing
our government, it would seem that we have voluntarily surrendered an important component of

our nationhood,'' write the Halifax Lawyers for Social Responsibility in their 1987 policy statement on the porting of nuclear-capable vessels in Canadian harbours.

I. Another Colony Heard From

But Mulroney and his cabinet see no breach or contradiction and maintain there is nothing inconsistent about nuclear-free Canada hosting somebody else's nuclear weapons at its docks. ''Canada does not possess any nuclear weapons, nor are there any on Canadian territory. But for Canada to declare itself to be a Nuclear Weapons Free Zone would be incompatible with our continued membership in NATO and NORAD,'' the Prime Minister explained in a 1984 letter to the Vancouver Island Network for Disarmament.

The Tories are not the only political party to fall back on the vacuous NATO alibi to explain their whereabouts on the nuclear warship issue. The Liberal Party spouts a similar line, although dresses it up somewhat before turning it loose on peace activists. ''We must uphold our traditional alliances,'' John Turner, Liberal party leader at the time, told the Nanoose Conversion Campaign in a 1988 letter. ''A Liberal government would work independently within NATO to promote peace. Hence, the transit of NATO nuclear vessels or aircraft through Canada would be the focus of serious discussion with our NATO allies by a Liberal government.'' Turner's oxymoronic quest to ''work independently within NATO'' is rivalled by his party's peculiar resolution, passed at a 1986 convention, to declare Canada a Nuclear Weapons Free Zone (NWFZ), but not at the expense of Canada's alliance obligations (i.e., America's nuclear navy can stay).

The New Democratic Party is the only major federal party keen to boot the nukes out of Canadian ports (and take a hike from NATO and NORAD while they're at it). New Democrat MPs have repeatedly raised the nuclear warship issue in the House of Commons, tabling numerous unsuccessful motions and petitions to keep US nukes out of Canadian water, soil and air.

Interestingly, a quick trip to the library reveals there is nothing in the NATO or NORAD agreements specifically requiring Canada to entertain another country's nuclear-armed warships at Nanoose or anywhere else. Canada's obligations under the North Atlantic Treaty are of a far more general character specifying "self help and mutual aid" and a call for all member nations to "unite their efforts for collective defence and for the preservation of peace and security." As for NORAD, the text of the North American Aerospace Defence agreement states that the treaty "is intended to assist the two Governments to develop and maintain their individual and collective capacity to resist air attack on their territories in North America in mutual self-defence." It takes some pretty clever reading to conclude that Canada is obliged under either of these agreements to host floating nuclear arsenals in its harbours.

When the Canadian government unveiled its new defence policy in 1987, it had learned to choose its words more carefully. Nuclear-capable warship visits were no longer a requirement of the NATO or NORAD agreements but merely a "logical consequence of our membership in an alliance and of our acceptance of the protection offered by collective defence." A year later, in a position paper titled

"Canada and Nuclear Weapons," the feds went one step further and acknowledged that going nuclear-free wouldn't automatically result in Canada's expulsion from NATO. "Declaring Canada a NWFZ would involve a serious abdication of our Alliance responsibilities and might require withdrawal from NATO," the government wrote.

II. No Nukes for the Grassroots

The federal government's commitment to preserving Canada's status as an American nuclear colony isn't stopping Canadians from going "nuclear free" in their own communities. Most Canadians recognize that NWFZ legislation at the municipal level is largely symbolic. However, what it symbolizes is popular sentiment—something federal politicians cannot afford to ignore for too long.

"Certainly this act is symbolic," Nanaimo alderman Owen Kennedy told his fellow councillors in May 1987 when he tabled a motion to designate this city of 50,000 people, located a few short kilometres from Nanoose Bay, a NWFZ. TV cameras and hot lights were trained on Kennedy. The audience gallery, normally half empty, was jammed with local peace activists who had come early enough to get a seat in chambers. The remainder occupied some hastily arranged overflow seating in the foyer and packed the wide staircase leading down to the ground floor.

"We don't expect that the voice of this council, or even the united voices of all the citizens here in Nanaimo, will bring instant and lasting peace." Frozen like a sea of statues, the overflow crowd strained to hear Kennedy's words crackling through the loudspeakers in the outer corridor. "This is but one step.

But the longest journey starts with one step. This step, joined by millions and even billions throughout the world, will make the first step on the moon pale to insignificance. For this is a first step away from nuclear madness and towards a global village.''

After some debate, Kennedy's motion carried, as have similar motions in scores of municipal councils around the country. Sixty percent of Canadians live in areas declared NWFZs by their local and provincial governments, including the provinces of Ontario and Manitoba, the Northwest Territories and more than 170 municipalities. Among those 170 are Vancouver, Victoria and CFMETR's two nearest towns: Nanaimo and Parksville. Each of the city councils for these communities passed NWFZ bylaws in the 1980s, beginning with Vancouver in 1983. But Ottawa stubbornly insists local governments and their puny bylaws don't have jurisdiction over the federal waters where the US Navy's nuclear warships are parked. ''The federal government does not recognize locally-declared NWFZs,'' the Department of External Affairs says.

So in April 1989, Vancouver city council passed a motion calling on Ottawa to declare Vancouver's port a NWFZ. Ottawa responded by reiterating its now-familiar dictum on nuclear-capable warships. ''Allowing such vessels to transit Canada's internal waters is an important element in Alliance cooperation,'' R.J. Lysyshyn of the Department of External Affairs wrote back. Despite the federal government's intransigence, the Sunshine Coast regional district on the BC mainland north of Vancouver subsequently demanded that Ottawa declare Georgia Strait and Nanoose Bay a NWFZ.

Meanwhile, on the southern tip of Vancouver

Island, eight out of ten municipalities have joined with the Greater Victoria Disarmament Group and the entire NDP caucus in the BC legislature to demand a federal environmental review of the hazards associated with porting nuclear warships. Under its own Order In Council, the federal government is obligated to conduct a public environmental assessment and review "if public concern about a proposal is such that a public review is desirable." Nevertheless, when Defence Minister of-the-day Bill McKnight received a deluge of review requests from the municipal councils, elected officials and peace and environmental groups in the greater Victoria area, he merely replied "I consider it imperative that Canada should continue to allow nuclear-propelled and nuclear-capable warships to visit our ports and waterways." What his successor Marcel Masse will do with the demand for a public environmental review of nuke ships remains to be seen.

III. You're Invited! Bring Your Own Spray Paint

Even the staid and conservative judiciary has begun to question Ottawa's policy on nuclear warship visits. When the USS *Independence*, a nuclear-capable aircraft carrier bearing a long and distinguished history of ten naval accidents, steamed into Vancouver harbour on August 9, 1989 (the forty-fourth anniversary of the US atomic bombing of Nagasaki), Greenpeace sent out its usual welcoming committee to greet the naval Goliath. Tiny rubber lifeboats buzzed the towering hulk as it tried to drop anchor, while Greenpeacers spray-painted radiation symbols on the hull and partially scaled a ladder up the mountain of steel. One protester even chained himself to the massive anchor chain to prevent it from being lowered. In keeping with the well-established tradition of warship protests in BC's nuclear triangle, the disarmers were eventually brought to heel and charged with mischief, while the warship parked its bombs and let the Stars and Stripes flap proudly in the breeze.

However, this time a funny thing happened in Vancouver provincial court when the defendants came to trial that December. After hearing the evidence, Judge Wallace Craig acquitted four of the accused and gave a conditional discharge to a fifth. Although the acquittal wasn't unprecedented, Judge Craig's stated reasons were. Boldly venturing into the political arena, Judge Craig said he found it "remarkable that the [federal] government sees fit to invite this type of equipment into Vancouver in view of the serious concerns people have about it . . . It almost invites protest."

But not even Vancouver, the so-called "peace capital of Canada" and birthplace of the now international Greenpeace organization, can claim citywide unanimity on the nuclear warship issue. The day after Judge Craig uttered his widely publicized decision and statement, the Vancouver Sea Festival Committee—bankrolled in part by Vancouver city council—announced it would continue to invite the US Navy's nuke-toters to the city's annual nautical bash.

IV. Just Say No

Not all citizens have such difficulty persuading their government to denuclearize their ports and waterways. On February 1, 1985, New Zealand Prime Minister David Lange refused to validate the USS

Buchanan's parking permit. The nuclear-capable Navy destroyer, which turned up at all three ports in BC's nuclear triangle during the 1980s, was scheduled to pay a port call to the South Pacific island country for military exercises the following month. The US State Department was not amused. Lange's impudent action was "a matter of grave concern which goes to the core of our mutual obligation as allies," the State Department announced ominously.

Lange stood firm. Eight months earlier his Labour Party had swept to power in the general elections on a strong anti-nuclear platform. The public that voted him in had made its views unmistakably clear on one point: New Zealanders didn't want nukes in their harbours.

"If the ship is nuclear-capable, it won't come unless we can be assured it does not carry nuclear arms," Lange informed Washington. His announcement left State Department officials grinding their molars, since no one in DC had any intention of confirming whether the *Buchanan*'s ASROC weapon system was on board and armed with nuclear warheads. As a conciliatory gesture, Lange added that he would welcome a visiting ship from New Zealand's ally "if the Americans would suggest a vessel that I know is not nuclear-armed." His offer did little to appease.

Fearing possible outbreaks of the Kiwi disease in other allied nations with similar anti-nuclear sentiments, the US realized it must act swiftly to show the world that no tiny, peacenik-infested island could challenge America's global nuclear prerogative and expect to get away unscathed. "Some Western countries have anti-nuclear and other movements which seek to diminish defence cooperation among the allied states," US State Department spokesman

Bernard Kalb warned. "We would hope that our response to New Zealand would signal that the course these movements advocate would not be cost-free in terms of security relationships with the United States."

In New Zealand's case, the price tag was expulsion from the 1951 Anzus mutual defence pact between the US, New Zealand and Australia. "New Zealand has basically taken a walk," US Secretary of State George Shultz told the Senate Budget Committee a couple of weeks after Lange just said no.

While Lange was riling the US administration, he was reaping accolades at home. Telegrams swamped his office at a rate of more than 1,000 per day expressing support for his nuclear ship ban. In Sweden, the Peace and Arbitration Society nominated him for the Nobel Peace Prize. Seven months later, on the fortieth anniversary of the US atomic bombing of Hiroshima, New Zealand joined seven other South Pacific nations including Australia in declaring the Pacific Ocean south of the equator a nuclear free zone—a goal that remains unfulfilled without the compliance of the nuclear navies.

In December 1985, Lange's government formalized his own country's nuclear ship ban by passing legislation barring nuclear-armed warships despite strong objections from Australia. (Interestingly, Australian Prime Minister Bob Hawke was one of the keenest proponents of the South Pacific nuclear-free zone pact earlier that year.) New Zealand's Labour government went down to defeat in the 1990 general elections due to worsening economic problems and the government's unpopular privatization program. However, the nuclear ship ban remains in effect under the country's current National party government.

More than two-thirds of Canadian voters want Canada to follow New Zealand's example and deny nuclear-armed warships entry to Canadian harbours, according to a 1988 Angus Reid poll. Given the recent disintegration of the Cold War, what is the reason behind Ottawa's anachronistic attempt to keep Canadian harbours nuclear-full? And what is the military's true agenda at Nanoose?

Chapter 4

JUST TESTING TORPEDOES?

The warships ply over the ocean
The subs we do not always see
But when they surface at Nanoose
They are a Nanoosance to me

Raging Grannies
(Tune: "My Bonnie Lies Over the Ocean")

During the months I was writing this book, I would occasionally surface (milk or toilet paper were the most common incentives) and bravely reacquaint myself with the universe, squinting into the daylight, eyes unable to endure anything brighter than the dull, amber glow of a VDT. Although I made every effort to seek out obscure, little supermarkets in the far reaches of town, my ghostly apparition would invariably collide with an acquaintance from my previous life as a human being. Inevitably, I would be called upon to account for my absence. It was no different this time. I had wedged my way between two unattended shopping carts when a familiar voice boomed out from behind me.

"G'day, Kim! So, you're still on this planet after all! Where've ya been hiding?"

No mistaking that salutation. I knew before I

turned around that it had to be Bill, my birdwatching pal from our local naturalist club.

"Bill. Hi. Book. I'm writing one. Uh... How are you?" I sputtered incoherently, having inadvertently unlearned the art of casual conversation during my prolonged stay in solitary.

"A book? Good on ya! Hey, am I in it?"

"Well, no," I began. "It's not that kind of a book." (Which proved to be a lie since here he is.) "Actually, it's about the military base at Nanoose and the US Navy's activities there..."

"The base? Why in a petunia's ear would you want to write about that?" (Bill's botanical expletives are one of his more unusual qualities.) "You know, Kim, they're just testing torpedoes up there."

Just testing torpedoes.

This is how many people living near Nanoose automatically describe the activities there. It is also the same response the government and military use in their attempts to placate public concern and queries about Nanoose. However, the "just testing torpedoes" assurance can only be stretched so far. It does not adequately explain why the US Navy is so interested in ASW research and how these weapons will be used.

I. First Strike and You're Out

According to Robert Aldridge, designer of the Trident and Polaris missile systems, people have good reason to worry about the larger implications of the US Navy's torpedo tests at Nanoose. For the Navy's ASW trials are an integral part of the so-called first strike strategy. Brought to you live and direct from four decades of Cold War, the first strike strategy refers to the plan to develop the ability to launch a pre-emptive attack that would destroy enough of the Soviet Union's strategic nuclear arsenal to reduce any retaliatory damage to "acceptable" levels.

The US government has consistently denied that it is pursuing this destabilizing military strategy. However, in his 1983 book *First Strike!*, Aldridge, who plied his trade at Lockheed Missiles and Space Company for sixteen years before resigning for reasons of conscience, attests to the unofficial but very real existence of a first strike strategy: "As I delved deeper into Pentagon activity I discovered a pattern more sinister than I had imagined. Evidence indicated that the Pentagon is looking far beyond what is needed for defense. It is developing the instruments which will allow the United States to fight and win a nuclear war, if survival after any type of nuclear conflict can be called a victory... Evolving technologies are putting this country in a position to launch a disabling and unanswerable first strike."

Anti-submarine warfare is a crucial component of the strategy because the United States would need to destroy virtually all of the Soviet Union's ballistic missile submarines in one blow to prevent the Soviet Union from striking back and inflicting unacceptable losses on the United States. By the Navy's own admission, a successful first strike is impossible so long as Soviet submarines are invulnerable. The other two legs of the strategic arsenal triad—ground-based and air-launched intercontinental nuclear weapons—are considerably easier to locate and obliterate in a rapid attack.

For these reasons, Aldridge, the Nanoose Conversion Campaign and others argue that the US Navy's program of ASW testing at Nanoose is profoundly destabilizing and jeopardizes international peace and security. Not only does it increase the likelihood that the United States will initiate nuclear war, it increases Soviet apprehensions about their own vulnerability, possibly prompting a "use it or lose it" strategy on their part.

"The first strike strategy is one of our most major concerns about Nanoose," Sunshine Goldstream of the Nanoose Conversion Campaign told me. "As they test these newer and more 'efficient' ways of killing, we are contributing in a very clear way to a continual build-up for a first strike capability, because the weapons tested at Nanoose are all first strike weapons."

Depending on whom you talk to, the Canadian government will at times insist that the Navy is merely testing defensive rather than offensive weapons systems at Nanoose. When queried about the offensive and destabilizing nature of the weapons testing at CFMETR, Prime Minister Brian Mulroney assured the Vancouver Island Network for Disarmament in 1984 that "Nanoose Bay is used jointly by Canada and the United States to test maritime defensive systems such as sonars, sonobuoys and torpedoes."

However, the answer I got from the director of defence relations for the External Affairs ministry is probably closer to the truth. "It is always difficult to state categorically whether a particular weapon is 'offensive' or 'defensive' in nature," John Fowell told me. "It is not facetious to suggest that the old maxim which states that the difference depends on whether one is holding the weapon or facing it, continues to be valid." Fowell denies any connection between the ASW trials at Nanoose and a first strike strategy.

But Fowell's former boss didn't equivocate on the defensive-vs.-offensive question. According to then External Affairs Minister Joe Clark, the ASW technology developed at Nanoose is not only defensive but "contributes to stability by providing a retaliatory option. Without it, consideration would have to be given to a launch-on-warning posture, given the vulnerability of land-based systems."

Aldridge is unimpressed by Clark's assertions. "Destroying Soviet missile-launching submarines during the conventional phase of armed conflict, as set forth in the US Navy's forward maritime strategy, is essential to a first strike capability," Aldridge told me. "Torpedoes fired by aircraft, surface ships and submarines, or delivered by rockets, are the main ASW weapon. Sonars and sonobuoys are needed to locate those submarine targets. In this sense, developing these weapons and sensors is aggressive, not defensive."

As for Clark's statement that without the ASW capability refined at Nanoose and elsewhere, the US would be forced to adopt a launch-on-warning posture, Aldridge says Clark has got things backward. "On the contrary, it is the nature of ASW, by supporting a US first strike, which could put the Soviets on a launch-on-warning stance," he said. "The only action that will reduce nuclear war risks," he added, "is to eliminate activity which supports a first strike stance on either side."

II. We're Bad, So Beat It

The first strike strategy and its essential ASW capability are linked to a larger, undisputed US military plan—namely, the forward maritime strategy.

During the eight years of Ronald Reagan's presidency, nuclear-capable warship visits to Canadian ports increased dramatically from a low of 90 ship-days in 1980 to an all-time high of 468 ship-days in 1986, according to DND documents obtained by Project Ploughshares and Operation Dismantle through the Access to Information Act. This surge in the US Navy's presence in Canada has been paralleled elsewhere around the globe and is part of the so-called "forward maritime strategy."

Implemented under Reagan, America's maritime strategy entails an aggressive policy of forward-basing US warships as close as possible to Soviet warships (particularly Soviet ballistic missile submarines) in and near their home waters. One of the stated intentions of the maritime strategy is to destroy, at the beginning of any conflict, all Soviet submarine-launched intercontinental ballistic missiles (i.e., the sea leg of the strategic arsenal triad), using conventional weapons such as non-nuclear torpedoes. Hence the Navy's keen interest in ASW testing at Nanoose.

"We will, at the first indication that conflict has started, start sinking Soviet submarines. We're going to get anything that's underwater and it's going to go as soon as we get ahold of it," Admiral Wesley L. McDonald, the retired Commander-in-Chief of the US Atlantic Fleet, explained in a 1986 article in *Air Force Magazine*. "They will try to do the same with us, but they are behind in ASW capability."

While the US fleet is roaming the globe during peacetime in search of imminent conflict, 85 percent of the Soviet submarine fleet is berthed, making it quite vulnerable to a US strike. The docked subs are easy targets for a rapid attack. But in order to make a clean sweep and prevent any submarine-launched ballistic missiles from reaching the United States, the US Navy will have to locate and sink the 15 percent of the Soviet sub fleet at sea.

"One of the most complex aspects of Phase II of the Maritime Strategy is anti-submarine warfare," writes US Admiral James Watkins, former chief of naval operations, in his paper describing the strategy. "It will be essential to conduct forward operations with attack submarines . . . As the battle groups move forward, we will wage an aggressive campaign against all Soviet submarines, including ballistic missile submarines."

As with the first strike strategy, the Canadian government also denies any involvement in the maritime strategy. In a 1989 letter to the Denman Island Peace Group, John Fowell of Canada's External Affairs Department insists "it is not Canadian policy to be involved in the USA's forward maritime strategy." Although it may not be policy, it certainly appears to be practice. And the ASW trials and sonobuoy testing at CFMETR are part of the script.

III. The More Things Change . . .

These circumstances form the basis for the argument that the US Navy's work at Nanoose is a microcosm of the larger pattern of Canadian compliance with and subordination to American military needs and interests—a situation leaving little room for national sovereignty or independent defence policy. As author Fred Knelman puts it in his book *America, God and the Bomb*: "Through its links to NORAD, NATO and its bilateral agreements, Canada has become a de facto nuclear colony of the Reagan Administration's war-fighting strategies.''

But is any of this relevant any more? The Warsaw Pact is history. East European countries are pursuing market-driven economies, and the Soviet Union—or what's left of it—is in political and economic disarray. Logic would dictate that the first strike strategy and the related maritime strategy have now been relegated to the history books.

Even before the Soviet Union's collapse in 1991, the US appeared to be switching from a defence policy inspired by MacArthur and McNamara to one inspired by McDonald's. Rather than nuke the Soviets into oblivion, America figured it would be easier to launch a Big Mac attack on Red Square and subsequently lobotomize Soviet citizens with endless re-runs of *Dallas* and *Love Boat*. (Hollywood producer Aaron Spelling generously decided to donate—not sell—these two mind-numbing TV series to Soviet Central Television. Apparently, Spelling is counting on Soviets, like their comrades in the liberated West, being more interested in discovering who shot JR than who shot JFK.)

But one should never underestimate the sluggishness of the military bureaucracy or mentality. Despite the near-total reconfiguration of the geopolitical landscape, it appears not much has changed in US naval strategy. In an April 1991 article mapping out the future role of the US maritime forces, Secretary of the Navy Lawrence Garrett III states: ''Our attack submarine force will retain the numbers and capability needed to hold at risk sea-based strategic platforms able to threaten the United States. We cannot discount the major open-ocean warfighting potential of the Soviet submarine force, which has yet to experience any downturn in production rates or technological developments. Threat of its use could reemerge quickly, should the intentions of the Soviet leadership change—so we can never afford to cede our current technological edge in submarines and anti-submarine warfare . . . The future may not be as different from the past as we once hoped it might be."

Garrett also stresses that the maritime strategy and the US policy of maintaining a "forward presence," including port calls to foreign countries, is still intact: "Forward deployment of naval forces in peacetime promotes regional stability by demonstrating continuity of commitment, strengthening friendships, enhancing readiness, and reducing reaction time in crises."

In July 1991, US military planners revised their nuclear war "targeting list," retaining 7,000 Soviet targets. According to US defence officials, the new list would enable the US to unload 5,000 warheads on the Russian republic alone—the site of most of the Soviet Union's strategic nuclear arsenal. The Cold War may be over, but apparently no one told the war planners. "It's not like cars where there's a new model every year," an official involved in revising the targeting list explained. "There's a lot of inertia in the system."

Bob Aldridge agrees. "The end of the Cold War hasn't ended the arms race," he told me in 1991 when I asked him about the current relevance of the first strike strategy and the Navy's work at Nanoose. "Until both countries (US and USSR) cut back to where a first strike capability is not possible, I still consider it a threat. ASW research is still going full speed as far as I can

determine.'' Peace activists witnessing the ASW testing at Nanoose would like to change that.

Chapter 5

ON THE PEACE TRAIL— DATELINE: NANOOSE

We know that it's hard for you Brian
But we think you ought to start tryin'
To give it your best
And tell the US
We want NO MORE SUBS!

Raging Grannies
(Tune: "Side By Side")

The sky loomed grey and formidable while the mercury hovered around zero degrees. Patches of crunchy snow mottled the roadside. And a heavy, wet cold clung like cobwebs to the sullen firs. But nothing could dampen the spirits of 300 people who, fuelled by their vision of a nonviolent world, set off on the first Remembrance Day peace walk to the Nanoose military base on November 11, 1984.

The four-kilometre strip of empty pavement slicing through the quiet, rural peninsula along the bay came alive that Sunday afternoon with song and colour. Curious residents peered out their front windows at the unexpected procession of banners, placards, parents pushing kids in strollers, and dogs trotting by wearing "No Nukes" T-shirts. The walkers strode unhurriedly down Powder Point Road, measuring their pace to a spontaneous round of "We Shall Overcome" and leaving hundreds of wispy white signatures hanging in the frosty air.

I kept up as best I could, juggling my radio gear, mike cords, two cameras, lenses, notepad, pen and miscellaneous shoulder bags, while fretting about how to get decent audio on the singing amid the squeaky stroller wheels. I knew there was a military base at the end of the road. And I knew a mob of peace marchers swarming outside the base on Remembrance Day, calling for an end to war and to the machinery of war, would make a good story. In 1984 that was all I knew.

After forty-five minutes we reached the entrance to the base and gathered on a grassy slope outside the unfenced boundary. In later years, DND would erect a chainlink fence topped with three strands of barbed wire. But for that first mass rally, a handful of base officials observed the speeches and songs apprehensively from behind some hastily placed sawhorses blocking the entrance.

Retired Lieutenant Colonel Woody Coward, a thirty-year veteran of the Canadian Armed Forces, came forward from the crowd and chillingly described his own exposure to nuclear weapons years earlier at the Nevada test site: "I stood on a Nevada desert hilltop at dawn. We turned our backs, closed our eyes, put our hands over our eyes, and when the bomb went off, I could see the bones in my hands." His left lapel sagged beneath the weight of nine medals dangling from bright ribbons. White hair framed a face etched by memories of the unthinkable. "Where is the logic in stockpiling 50,000 nuclear warheads when 400 are enough to obliterate the world?" he asked. "Where is the humanity when weapons have a higher priority than feeding the hungry and alleviating suffering all over the globe?''

After Coward's speech, fifty people lay down on the cold, hard pavement leading into the base and remained as lifeless as the dank asphalt beneath them for a ten-minute Die-In. ''The Die-In symbolizes what would happen if one of the nuclear weapons carried into Nanoose were to detonate,'' the organizers wrote in their hand-out to the walkers. ''Please feel free to participate or to join us in silent prayer.''

Although few of us recognized it at the time as we stood there with our cheeks tingling and our fists jammed deep in pockets, we were, on that chill November afternoon, witnessing a birth. For it was here at this moment, in the skin-prickling cold with each breath sucking in the damp, coastal air, that the Nanoose Conversion Campaign was born.

I. You Can't Hide

The 1984 Nanoose peace walk wasn't the first display of public protest to the military activities at Nanoose Bay. On January 20, 1973, while Richard Nixon was being sworn in for his second term as president, the Vancouver Island Peace Company staged a mass rally across the bay from the Nanoose base protesting Canadian complicity in the Vietnam war. Huddled under an enormous, billowing canopy to escape lashing winds and rain, more than sixty people passed through the all-day encampment on the beach, warming their bellies with hot chocolate and their hands and feet beside a huge bonfire. At dusk, with MP Tommy Douglas among the cocoa-sippers, the protesters torched a model of the Pentagon (which had served as a garbage can throughout the day). Later that night, more than two dozen people drove into the base and plastered it with posters of the Vietnamese flag.

Defence officials were bewildered by the protest and midnight invasion. Those "confused" and "slightly misinformed" peaceniks had made a muddle out of geopolitics once again, CFB Esquimalt's Major Vic Keating subsequently told reporters. Didn't they know Nanoose was only a torpedo testing station? "Not one torpedo has been fired in Vietnam by the US. The water over there is too shallow for torpedo use," the major assured the press.

But for the protesters, the connection between CFMETR and America's bloody adventure in southeast Asia was as deep and clear as the crystalline waters of Georgia Strait. "The Nanoose rally was one of hundreds of Inauguration Day demonstrations around the world expressing revulsion at the farce of the October 31 peace hopes and the Christmas bombing of Hanoi and Haiphong," Nanoose resident Deeno Birmingham wrote in a Parksville newspaper the following week. "Like others in our own country, [the Nanoose rally] protested Canadian complicity in the war, and for the central Vancouver Island area it was entirely appropriate that the focus should be on the nearest example of US-Canadian military co-operation."

Sporadic on-site protests to the US Navy's presence and research at Nanoose continued. In 1982, the newly formed Vancouver Island Network for Disarmament (VIND) launched a twenty-ship flotilla, which sailed over to the Nanoose base and dispatched a landing party to deliver a prepared statement to the base commander calling for a nuclear-free Vancouver Island: "... CFMETR is directly implicated as an integral part of the US Navy weapons system which now has at its disposal a first strike capability . . . This is an unprecedented threat to life on earth. To be part of that military network violates the Nuremberg Accord of 1946 which declares the preparation for war illegal . . . As citizens of Vancouver Island, we desire security through the creation of a Nuclear Weapons Free Zone in this area. The continued use of the CFMETR facilities at Nanoose Bay makes this security impossible.''

The statement revealed a maturation in the opposition to the Nanoose base by connecting the US Navy's ASW trials at CFMETR to the first strike strategy, violations of international law and risks to local public safety. But it was still just one isolated protest action.

Deciding that dialogue with the public would be more productive than unanswered monologue with the government, VIND began parking an old, blue pick-up truck in a rest stop along the island highway across the bay from CFMETR. For three summers, VIND members dispensed coffee, leaflets and conversation to thousands of travellers cruising past the deceptively peaceful bay. But it wasn't until the first Remembrance Day Nanoose peace walk in 1984 that a grassroots resistance of a more lasting nature was born.

II. All We Are Saying

Organizers of the 1984 walk unveiled the Nanoose Conversion Campaign at the rally and read out a three-point resolution defining the goals of the campaign. The resolution was endorsed by all and wired later that day to recently elected Prime Minister Brian Mulroney. It went:

> Whereas Canada should be promoting a lessening of world tensions instead of contributing to a dangerous escalation of the arms race, we are resolved to achieve:
>
> 1. non-renewal of the Canada–US treaty governing the use of the Nanoose testing range when it expires in April 1986;
> 2. an end to all weapons testing at CFMETR;
> 3. conversion of CFMETR to peaceful purposes.

Mulroney was just two months into his new job as Canada's PM, so perhaps it wasn't surprising that his assistant thanked the peace walkers for their "resolution on nuclear disarmament," even though their telegram made no mention of nuclear disarmament. Dismayed by the apparent lack of reading skills in the Prime Minister's office, the peace walkers wrote back to Mulroney reiterating their original three-point resolution about CFMETR and suggesting that "the credibility of your government will be enhanced when replies to communications are relevant."

The organizers had initially planned on waging a twenty-month campaign, to be capped by a victory celebration in 1986 when the treaty was deep-sixed. When 1986 rolled around and the treaty was renewed for another ten years, the campaigners were forced to revamp their timetable—but not their aspirations. To this day, the campaign's agenda remains remarkably unchanged from what it started out as on that cold afternoon in November. The NCC is now seeking:

> 1. to cancel the Canada-US agreement governing the use of CFMETR;

2. to end all weapons testing in the Georgia Strait;
3. to convert CFMETR to peaceful, productive purposes.

A week before the inaugural peace walk, the fledgling group settled on its name. "We needed to open a bank account before the walk, because we knew we would be taking a collection that day. So we had to come up with a name," NCC co-founder Laurie MacBride recalled. Among the contenders were: Nanoose Peace Campaign, Nanoose Action for Peace, Committee for a Peaceful Nanoose, and even STING—Stop Testing In Nanoose Group. But the founders, a collection of eight Vancouver Island peace activists who wanted to draw public attention to Nanoose through direct action, settled on Nanoose Conversion Campaign because it identified their work in positive and specific terms. "Hendrik came up with the name," Laurie explained, referring to co-founder Hendrik deWilde. "Conversion was a fairly new concept at the time. Hendrik said it was important to be seen as going for something positive and not just being against things."

From the outset, the NCC has been keenly committed to a philosophy and practice of nonviolence. The second word in the group's name refers not only to the economic conversion of CFMETR, but to a personal conversion of consciousness and a collective conversion of society. An interesting internal debate erupted four years later when some NCCers organized thirty people to "shell" the Nanoose base with oyster shells to protest Canada's participation in an international military exercise (RIMPAC) which regularly shells a sacred Hawaiian island. Base officials were more puzzled than fazed by the pelting near the dock. But other NCC members opposed the action, saying it was violent and combative in concept since it simulated a military assault.

The original members were strongly influenced by the anti-authoritarian, decentralist, eco-feminist and "green" philosophical currents that have been sweeping through activist politics and the social change movement in Canada and elsewhere since the early 1980s. To this day, NCCers make all decisions by consensus rather than a majority vote technique. Until 1991, the campaign has never had a board of directors or a central co-ordinator but has relied instead on various committees, open to anyone, to carry out specific tasks.

In the early months following the 1984 peace walk, the eight founders and a handful of newcomers took charge of the care and feeding of the campaign. What they lacked in resources, they made up for with enthusiasm, determination and commitment to their vision of a nuclear-free and converted Nanoose. As I got to know them, I discovered they were parents, tree planters, teachers, poets, youth workers. They were people who valued the natural beauty and serenity of their island life and who had a long-standing commitment to working for peace. One member, Laurie MacBride, ultimately gave up her teaching position at a local middle school to devote herself full-time to the campaign.

"Learning that sea-launched cruise missiles were coming into Nanoose Bay really brought the whole issue home for me," Laurie recalled. "Up until then, I had been curious about Nanoose, but I didn't really know much about it. At that time [1984] we were all busy protesting cruise missile testing over Alberta, and here was the cruise coming into my own backyard, five miles away from where I lived. People weren't willing to believe it at first. Also, learning that the treaty was up for renewal gave me something to hope for."

In June 1984, the US Navy began deploying nuclear-armed Tomahawk sea-launched cruise missiles (SLCMs) on certain classes of surface ships and submarines. Eleven months later, NCC members (who had begun maintaining a ceaseless vigil of the base's nuclear visitors) logged their first positive sighting of a Tomahawk-packing sub in local waters. "One of our worst fears came true," the campaigners announced in their inaugural newsletter, *Nanoose Update* (which became a monthly commodity for conversion supporters and an important outreach tool for the campaign). "The *La Jolla*, a Los Angeles class nuclear submarine, visited Nanoose. This sub is one of 15 positively identified as carrying Tomahawk cruise missiles, some of which are nuclear-capable. Other subs and ships will be armed with nuclear Tomahawks in the very near future as this weapon is emerging as the most important new development in the US arsenal. We issued a press release immediately . . . The Vancouver *Sun* and *Province* did not release the story to their readers, and the CBC declined to run it unless they could get footage of the sub. Only the community papers expressed interest. Where's Clark Kent now that we need him?"

The nuclear-armed Tomahawk SLCM has a range of 2,500 kilometres and a variable explosive power of 5–150 kilotons. By way of comparison, the atomic bomb the US dropped on Hiroshima had an explosive force of 20 kilotons. The Tomahawk SLCM also comes in a conventionally armed version. Tomahawk-certified attack submarines are each assumed to be carrying a mixed load of nuclear and conventional Tomahawks. Although not tested at Nanoose, the US cruise missiles aboard the Navy's combat-ready attack subs were yet another deadly indication to the conversion advocates that Nanoose Bay was nothing more than a branch plant of US War Inc., whose CEO was Ronald Reagan.

III. Boot Camp Days for the NCC

Early on, the NCC decided it needed a visible and permanent presence somewhere near the base, both to keep an eye on the subs and to draw public attention to the issue and the site. On April 1, 1985, an encampment of tipis and tents sprang up in a small, rural park along Powder Point Road about a mile from the base. The base commander, who had been forewarned of his new neighbours, dropped by the campsite long enough to compliment the peace activists on their punctuality.

The NCC tipis weren't the only large objects popping up on the Nanoose landscape that April Fool's Day. While the disarmers pounded tent pegs, the USS *Pintado*, a nuclear-powered attack submarine certified to carry the SUBROC nuclear weapon system, slithered into the bay. The *Pintado* (which some years earlier had crashed into a Soviet sub and a Korean Navy ship in two separate fender benders on the other side of the globe) spent the next three days at dock and out on the test range. The tipis were more enduring. Although relocated twice due to relentless bureaucratic bullying, the Nanoose Peace Camp, as it came to be known, hung in for 466 days.

The campers may not have suspected it in the early days, but their conical tipis silhouetted against the skyline would become a potent icon of grassroots resistance to the clandestine forces of a global military machine. The image of the peace camp tipis has been reproduced on postcards and literature circulated across North America and Europe. But daily life at the peace camp nestled in the salal and arbutus was more often humbling than glorifying.

"Finally we practiced some nudity in the camp today," Hendrik wrote in the camp log book one month after the tipis went up. "But suddenly two passers-by showed up wanting to use the plastic shithouse. Despite our earlier bragging that we would like to receive the official world without a thread, we quickly dressed when it came down to the nitty gritty of fulfilling our boast."

Three months and two moves after it first appeared, the camp was finally installed in a prominent spot along the Island highway across the bay from the base and very near the VIND peace truck parked at the rest stop. From their high-visibility shoreline campsite, the campers weathered a cold, wet, muddy winter wrestling with soaked sleeping bags, frozen dish towels, flagging spirits and, at times, a foot of snow.

"Four adults and three children were at the peace camp to celebrate the birth of the new year," the campers wrote in their first newsletter of 1986. "The sound of the traffic was drowned out by the high tide crashing against the beach and the stiff wind and rain drumming against the tipi canvas. By the light of the kerosene lamp and candles we drank the health of the Nanoose camp which has now survived 275 days."

While the campers were preoccupied with scrounging firewood, lamps, tarps and pallets, the non-camping public in the surrounding communities was debating the merits of the soggy tipis and what they stood for. Some viewed the campers as an inspirational testament to citizens' ability and right to protest. "Those peace campers are the only people anywhere who are consistently and actively doing something specific to deal with the greatest single threat there is to our local well being, and indeed our very lives, here in the Nanaimo–Parksville area," Reverend Peter Horsfield wrote in a Nanaimo paper. And from a local college instructor: "Rather than feeling anger and resentment toward these people, we should treat those who work for peace with the respect we have always given to soldiers fighting for a cause . . . I believe the soldiers of today are those who fight to prevent nuclear war, and to avert suffering on a scale unimaginable to any of us," Ross Fraser wrote in another local paper.

But others accused them of trespassing, illegally camping, maintaining improper toilet facilities, marring the scenery, living off the avails of the state and even threatening national security. "We can thank our lucky stars that Uncle Sam, our wonderful godfather, came up with the hydrogen bomb when he did," James Dougan wrote in a Parksville paper. "You fools. Don't you understand? The only reason we're safe is because our close proximity to a friendly giant with plenty of missiles and warheads keeps us safe." And from M.G. Williams writing in the Nanaimo *Times*: "Why do we allow this to go on? It's disgusting and a very dirty eyesore— gets more so every day. Looks like a camp along the tracks in the early thirties. There is no good lesson or example set here, just a dirty camp and a bunch of freeloaders in it."

The dirty eyesore debate apparently struck some people's funny bone. "I don't mind having nuclear warheads in my neighbourhood," Parksville resident "I. Rate" said in a letter published in a local paper. "They are stylish and neatly painted. The conversion camp members are another matter. Why are these hippies wasting their time instead of amassing money, power and prestige like normal people? Don't get me wrong—I love humanity; but I can't stand anyone who doesn't look, think or act the same as me."

Although steadfast in their commitment to their cause, the campers were not immune to the demoralizing effect of negative feedback from a public they had hoped would join them at least in spirit if not body. "We sometimes wish that local residents would give us more encouragement. We seem to be better known internationally than at the local level," one unidentified camper wrote in the peace camp's daily log book. And from another signed only as 'B': "I find it painfully amusing that the residents who object to our presence at the camp do not feel similar misgivings about nuclear-powered and nuclear-loaded attack subs. I wonder why we appear more threatening. Familiarity breeds complacence, apparently."

Schlepping firewood and dodging flak were not the only pastimes NCCers engaged in during the early phase of their campaign. The members had been cranking out a monthly newsletter with a circulation approaching 300; touring western Canada, Ontario, Washington and Oregon with a slide show; staffing an office in Nanaimo; researching environmental hazards associated with nuclear warship visits; and doing some heavy political lobbying, collecting many thousands of signatures on petitions. The petition drive culminated in the entire federal New Democrat caucus spending weeks presenting the petitions in the House of Commons, while New Democrat MP Jim Manly tabled a private member's bill calling for a government enquiry into CFMETR before the treaty was renewed in 1986.

While the campers were huddled in their tipis amid freezing winter rains, a significant event was unfolding in Nanaimo—an event that catapulted the campaign to national and international prominence. In January 1986, another local peace group, the Gabriola Island Peace Association, staged the People's Enquiry into CFMETR—a project the group undertook after seeing the NCC's travelling slide show the previous year. To the delight and astonishment of the organizers (if not the fire marshal), more than 500 people from across Canada turned out for the two-day enquiry in Nanaimo moderated by Bishop Remi De Roo of Victoria and by publisher Mel Hurtig, who flew out from Edmonton. Doctors, scientists, university professors, lawyers, labour leaders and independent researchers delivered papers on CFMETR's impact on the marine environment, Canadian sovereignty, public safety, the economy, international relations and a host of other related topics. For its part, the NCC presented a paper on the feasibility of conversion—a paper which gave many people their first glimpse of the CFMETR facility as something other than a US nuke station.

In the months preceding the enquiry, the organizers repeatedly beseeched CFMETR, DND and the federal government to send someone to present the government's point of view. In all cases the invitations were ignored or declined. Ultimately there was no government representation either in the audience or among the speakers. Even Ted Schellenberg, the Conservative MP for the riding, was a no-show due, he claimed, "to a very hectic schedule and previous parliamentary commitments," despite being invited five months in advance. The same, however, was not true of the media. The People's Enquiry was covered by all major Canadian media, including the Canadian Press wire service, as well as Britain's BBC. At last Nanoose Bay, churning with the America's nuclear navy, was unmistakably and forever on the map.

Support for the Nanoose Conversion Campaign grew astronomically after the enquiry. The NCC's mailing list for its monthly newsletter doubled to 600 names, prompting a flood of cash donations in response to funding pleas. More people started showing up at the peace camp with sleeping bags, firewood and hot meals. The stalwart band of campers, who had in most cases forsaken income and the luxury of a warm home, were no longer alone.

The bureaucratic machinations that ultimately dislodged the peace camp were spearheaded by the Regional District of Nanaimo. The landowner of the peace camp's turf was CIP Inc., a subsidiary of Canadian Pacific Rail. (The tipis were sitting on a CPR right-of-way.) CIP wasn't highly motivated to move against the squatters, but when the Regional District of Nanaimo threatened to prosecute CIP for violating an obscure zoning bylaw involving inadequate toilets, the company eventually evicted them.

The NCC members mourned the loss of their camp, which had taken on an almost spiritual role as a beacon of hope and determination for their cause. But they recognized they had to stay focussed on the primary issue of US weapons testing at Nanoose Bay and could not afford to dissipate their energies and scarce funds defending their right to live without portable toilets.

"This is not an easy decision for us, and we are certainly sad to be losing the peace camp," the NCC wrote in its newsletter July 10, 1986, the day the tipis came down. "It has been an important focal point for the campaign and a place for us to learn and grow together... [But] it seems to us that fighting CIP right now would be counter-productive to our long-term goals. Our concern is with CFMETR, not CIP."

The lapping surf gently spoke its goodbyes under a mid-summer sun while the peace campers glumly dismantled their canvas condos and disappeared down the highway. One month earlier, the Canada–US agreement governing the use of CFMETR had been renewed for another ten-year period. "We're not beaten at all," Michael Justice told me as he pushed the last wheelbarrow load of bedding and kitchen supplies up the slope to the highway shoulder and added it onto the heap in the back of his pick-up truck. All that remained in the clearing along the shore was one empty tipi and the pole skeleton of another. "It's just a matter of changing our tactics," he said, lashing down the remnants of fifteen months of hope, dreams and subsistence living. "We're as determined as ever to have the treaty cancelled and have Nanoose converted to peaceful and productive uses."

IV. A Long-term Lease on Peace

Although the NCCers originally believed their campaign would halt the 1986 treaty renewal, the members gradually came to realize it would take more than a year-long camp-out to shred the treaty which had been in force since 1965. "We fully expected its renewal, having realized that creating the political will for termination of the agreement is a long-term process," they wrote the day they broke camp.

"We feel that for the short year and a half the NCC has existed, we are well along the road to creating that will. And we are determined and committed to keep the process going. With the continued patient and persistent efforts of all of us, we will get the Nanoose agreement terminated and eventually see the area converted to peaceful, productive purposes."

The dismantling of the peace camp forced the members to develop a long-term strategy. "The next two months will be an important transition phase for us," NCC members wrote. "We feel something positive, creative and effective can grow out of this change. The Chinese character that represents 'crisis' also translates as 'opportunity.'"

True to their prophecy, the NCC's transitional phase lasted exactly two months, and a major opportunity did emerge out of their crisis of homelessness. In September 1986, a Saltspring Island couple, who took up the NCC's cause after attending the People's Enquiry, purchased a small, grey cottage overlooking Nanoose Bay and the military dock on the far shore. They agreed to lease the tiny abode to the NCC for a nominal sum, and this unobtrusive dwelling became the Nanoose Peace House: long-term home to the Nanoose Conversion Campaign plus meeting space cum drop-in centre for peace and social justice groups up and down Vancouver Island.

The campaign had previously rented a small, hole-in-the-wall office in Nanaimo that was closed more often than open. The new house allowed the group to finally organize its massive files, to establish a lending library and to run a clearinghouse for all campaign activities. In the pre-house days, the NCC initiated several research and letter-writing committees on environmental issues (relating to CFMETR), conversion, political lobbying and other topics as the need arose. With the acquisition of the house, the work and results of these committees became accessible to everyone. Today the peace house contains an impressive database and public resource centre boasting hundreds of files, books and pamphlets on naval vessels, their weapons, anti-submarine warfare, forward maritime strategy, US and Canadian defence policies, the legality of nuclear weapons, radiation hazards, nuclear emergency planning, other conversion projects in Canada and abroad, nonviolence training, social defence, "paradigm shifting," consensus decision making and much more.

Various NCC members and supporters have taken turns living in the house over the years, faithfully maintaining the vigil with a spotting scope permanently trained on the military dock across the bay. A spacious addition was constructed in the summer of 1987, transforming the cramped cottage into a popular venue for groups, workshops, touring speakers, visiting peace activists from other countries and a series of Thursday night public talks on peace issues. All this activity brought in new members and resources for the NCC and helped to integrate the local campaign with the broader peace movement regionally and beyond.

The Remembrance Day Nanoose peace walk, begun in 1984, has become an annual event drawing between 250 and 400 people most years. The NCCers have travelled to peace conferences in Canada, the US and abroad to share information about their campaign. As a result of the NCC's persistent effort to highlight the risks posed by nuclear warships, a growing number of local governments within

BC's nuclear triangle are demanding (to little avail so far) adequate nuclear emergency response plans for their areas or, better still, a ban on nuclear ship visits. In a phrase, the campaign has taken root.

However, nothing lasts forever. The peace house owners plan to put the house up for sale in 1992. "While the peace house has become an old familiar friend to many of us and we will miss it, this is an opportunity for the campaign to make itself visible and move forward in new ways," the NCC told supporters in a newsletter. As of September 1991, the campaign was reorganizing and, contrary to the group's earlier anarchist tendencies, established a board of directors. Members conducted a major fund-raising drive in the summer of 1991 with the intention of opening a storefront office in Nanaimo and, for the first time in the NCC's history, hiring a campaign co-ordinator.

The public inspects a Canadian naval vessel docked at the Nanoose base on the Annual Open House Day. Photo by Kim Goldberg.

A Mark-48 torpedo, one of the weapons tested at Nanoose. Photo by Michael Justice, courtesy of the Nanoose Conversion Campaign.

A US Navy nuclear-powered and nuclear weapons capable attack submarine visits Nanoose for anti-submarine warfare trials. Photo courtesy of the Nanoose Conversion Campaign.

Nanoose base commander Dan McVicar (left) and base administration officer Ken Casson (right). Photo by Kim Goldberg.

Base officials and military police await the Motherpeace Eight as the women attempt to land on North Winchelsea Island, the command centre for the base's anti-submarine warfare trials. Photo courtesy of the Nanoose Conversion Campaign.

The Motherpeace Eight on the courthouse steps after their acquittal on January 15, 1987. Back row, left to right: Carole Roy, Nina Westaway. Middle row: Liberty Bradshaw, Betty Fairbank, Laurie MacBride. Front row: Sunshine Goldstream, Anne Lindsay, Miriam Leigh. Photo by Kim Goldberg.

Nanoose Conversion Campaign supporters hold a chilly vigil outside a Parksville courthouse in January 1987, while the Motherpeace Eight stand trial for trespassing. Middle: Rev. Peter Horsfield; right: John Broderick. Photo by Kim Goldberg.

Bishop Remi De Roo of Victoria moderates Day One of the People's Enquiry into CFMETR, held in Nanaimo in January 1986. Photo by Don Furnell.

Trident missile designer Robert Aldridge, at the People's Enquiry into CFMETR, testifies on the offensive and destabilizing nature of anti-submarine warfare research. Photo by Kim Goldberg.

Brian Mills, a founding member of the Nanoose Conversion Campaign and the only one of nineteen Mobilization for Survival arrestees to stand trial, was acquitted on a technicality. Photo by Kim Goldberg.

For two months following the dismantling of the peace camp, the Nanoose Conversion Campaign operated out of a fifty-foot junk moored in Nanoose Bay. Photo by Kim Goldberg.

William Arkin, a former US Army intelligence analyst and currently Greenpeace consultant and co-author of the Neptune Papers series, has been one of many visitors to the Nanoose Peace House over the years. Photo by Kim Goldberg.

Veterans Against Nuclear Arms members at the annual Remembrance Day Nanoose Peace Walk. At right is (retired) Lt. Col. Woody Coward, the keynote speaker at the first Nanoose peace walk on November 11, 1984. Photo by Kim Goldberg.

A tipi across the road leading to the base has been a frequent tactic of the Nanoose Conversion Campaign. Photo by Kim Goldberg.

Participants in the annual Remembrance Day peace walk at Nanoose conclude each walk by hanging symbols of life on the chainlink fence at the main entrance to the base. Photo by Kim Goldberg.

Local peace activists were surprised and moved when Nanoose base commander Dan McVicar, his wife Denise and their three young daughters joined in a round of seasonal songs at a December 1989 vigil outside the base gates. Photo by Kim Goldberg.

Chapter 6

EXCUSE ME, YOUR
HONOUR, BUT . . .

It isn't nice to block the roadway
It isn't nice to go to jail
There are nicer ways to do it
But the nice ways often fail.

Raging Grannies
(Tune: original)

Vigorous gusts of wind whipped the hot summer air across the bay dotted with whitecaps atop two-foot swells. But the bobbing flotilla of sailboats, canoes and a kayak would not be turned back on August 3, 1986. Not even when the tiny craft rounded the mouth of the bay and were tossed into the choppier waters of Georgia Strait.

"I'm doing this because I'm so frustrated," Miriam told me on shore before she and seven other women scrambled unsteadily into their rickety wooden dinghies and rowed out to board the *Gust O'*. "I'm fearful for my children and the children of the world."

And she was. I could hear the fear in her voice. A hundred yards away, two large tipis from the old Nanoose peace camp (dismantled one month earlier) had been resurrected for the weekend. Dozens of supporters, some coming from as far away as Seattle and Portland, puttered around the camp, while kids and dogs chased each other through the underbrush.

After forty-five minutes of pitching and rolling, with a thin layer of crusty salt coating lips and eyeglasses, the flotilla approached a small patch of beach on Winchelsea Island, the command centre for the anti-submarine warfare trials. Five dark-suited military officials stood impassively at the ocean's edge as the eight-woman landing party rowed ashore in their four tiny dinghies, dancing like walnut shells in the heaving surf. "We nearly lost a couple of rowers," Sunshine recalls.

"At first they were shoving me back, not letting me come on the island," Anne said when she returned. "They told us they'd have to arrest us if we didn't leave." But no struggle ensued. Even without DND's help, the determined sailors in the all-woman peace navy stood a good chance of winding up in the salt chuck while trying to disembark from their puny craft. So the military officials opted for a flexible response. They allowed the women to clamber ashore and carry out their symbolic reclamation of the island.

Under a cornflower-blue sky, the Motherpeace Eight, as the media later dubbed them, stood in a circle on the rocky beach and, clutching the edge of a white tablecloth snapping in the wind, passed an "apple of wisdom" from mouth to mouth, each taking a bite.

"A guard kept tying to grab the apple as we were passing it," Liberty recounted. "But he was nearly bitten and became embarrassed."

"How symbolic!" Sunshine added.

Rhythmic as the slapping surf, the military police, with guns holstered at their hips, moved around the circle beneath the jeering gulls and lightly touched each woman on the shoulder to signify she had been informed of her arrest. As the militia played out their solemn ballet, the words of an anthem made famous at the women's peace camp at Britain's Greenham Common rose up from the circle and fluttered away across indigo waters on the warm, summer wind:

> You can forbid nearly everything
> But you can't forbid us to think
> And you can't forbid our tears to flow
> And you can't shut our mouths when we
> sing.

With the Motherpeace ritual and the police's parallel ritual completed, the women headed back to their beached dinghies—but not without first offering a gift of potted herbs to their arresters, who soberly refused the subversive green sprigs. "We also left crystals and amethysts on the beach," Liberty recalls. "A symbol of the psychic and spiritual bond to the earth and to Winchelsea—an act of reclaiming and healing. Some of us tried to draw women's symbols and healing symbols on the rock beach with a piece of shale. A guard with rubber-soled, military-issued boots jumped on one of the symbols and tried to erase it with his scuffing. He yelled at us that our drawings were destructive to property. One of us asked him if using the Georgia Strait for testing missiles wasn't."

As the women shoved their unstable dinghies into the aggressive surf and tried to board without capsizing, the police watched anxiously from the shore and asked if they would be able to make it back all right. "They were obviously concerned about our safety," Laurie told me later back at the camp. "It was pretty rough out there."

I. Dances with Subs

The Motherpeace action was not the NCC's first stab at civil disobedience, although it was the first to land the group in court. One year earlier, in September 1985, the members had added nonviolent civil disobedience to their campaign strategy after growing increasingly disillusioned and frustrated with the lack of results their more law-abiding methods were netting.

"It is becoming clear that the Canadian government has no intention of taking any peace initiative on its own, so the people must act if progress is to be made in curbing the arms race," the group wrote in its newsletter that month. "The NCC would like to contact anyone who would like to take part in [arrest risking] actions, but only those people with a firm commitment to non-violence will be included."

Later that month, the USS *Salt Lake City* snorkeled into the bay, and the campaign decided to put its bodies where its mouth was. Six NCCers delivered a letter to base officials requesting the removal of the nuclear-powered attack submarine, then hunkered down on the road in front of the main gate. A throng of media and NCC supporters hovered around the human blockade for most of the afternoon. But the savvy base security team waited patiently until it grew dark and the media had gone home before calling in the RCMP to arrest and remove the blockaders. All charges were later dropped.

The pattern was set. Over the next three years, US nuclear sub visits to Nanoose were punctuated by road blockades, sea blockades, early morning skirmishes between police cruisers and rubber life boats, unapproved picnics, sing-ins and occasionally a portable tipi blocking the main entrance. More than fifty arrests were made during that time. However, charges were later dropped in all but two of the incidents, allowing CFMETR and the government to neatly avoid the muss and fuss of public trials. The Crown's bashfulness about prosecuting the peaceniks irked some local residents.

"How much longer are Crown prosecutors going to continue to sanction the abuse the military takes from the Commie-inspired rabble at Nanoose?" Nanaimo newspaper editor Merv Unger asked one week in his editorial. "No matter how many charges police lay, Crown prosecutors continue to drop charges. It appears almost as though the prosecutors have assumed the role of judge and jury in these cases. How about letting the duly appointed judges rule on the guilt and punishment of lawbreakers?"

Unfortunately for Unger and others who share his sentiments, the duly appointed judges who did finally rule on the guilt and punishment of NCC members acquitted the "rabble" in each case. Even the NCC didn't rejoice with gay abandon over these acquittals, for they were won on technicalities, not the potentially precedent-setting defence the group's lawyer had devised.

The 1945 Charter of the International Military Tribunal (IMT) states that "planning, preparation, initiation or waging of a war of aggression" constitutes a crime against peace, and that "leaders, organizers, instigators and accomplices . . . are responsible for all acts performed by any persons in execution of such plan." Twenty-two of Nazi Germany's political, military and economic leaders were indicted and tried in Nuremberg, Germany, under this and other clauses contained in the IMT charter. Canada is a signatory to the charter, whose clauses regarding crimes against peace, war crimes and crimes against humanity have come to be known in international law as the Nuremberg Principles.

The NCC maintains that, because of the link between ASW and first strike strategy, the testing at Nanoose is, in fact, preparation for waging a war of aggression, thereby giving citizens the legal right and duty to disobey domestic laws in an effort to halt activities that are illegal under international law.

In addition to the Nuremberg Principles, NCC members plan to invoke the Canadian Charter of Rights and Freedoms in defence of their actions. Section 7 of the Charter offers them their best shot, stating "Everyone has the right to life, liberty and security of the person and the right not to be deprived thereof except in accordance with the principles of fundamental justice." The NCC figures the presence of nuclear-powered, nuclear-capable vessels at Nanoose certainly threatens the lives and security of local inhabitants. The campaigners also argue that the ASW testing done at Nanoose threatens the lives and security of all Canadians since it increases the likelihood of war. Other sections of the Charter, such as Section 2 guaranteeing freedom of conscience and belief, may also be tried out in court by the NCC if the opportunity arises.

II. Tricky Tide Tables

Sixteen months after the NCC embarked on its campaign of civil disobedience, the group finally got its first crack at the judicial system. The Motherpeace Eight, charged with trespassing on DND property from their 1986 escapade, turned up in a tiny Parksville courtroom the following January to defend their actions before a poker-faced magistrate. Anxious supporters packed the cramped chambers, sitting two to a chair and spilling into the hall, while outside in near-freezing temperatures an additional fifty campaign backers, clutching candles in mittened hands, maintained a silent vigil and awaited the word.

I was so busy interviewing supporters outside before the trial began, that I was lucky to get a seat. "Here, take my place, Kim. It's very important that the press be here," Summer said when she saw I was about to be ushered out of the chambers with the rest of the overflow crowd. I felt guilty sending an eighty-year-old woman out into a frigid January morning to huddle with the others on the sidewalk. But I couldn't afford to miss the guts of the story, and there was only one place to be for that.

Tim Leadem, the NCC's lawyer and master chef of the campaign's great unheard defence, planned to call various expert witnesses to establish that ship visits and the weapons testing at Nanoose posed a threat to the local inhabitants and constituted preparation for war. Trident missile designer Robert Aldridge flew up from California to testify on the offensive role of ASW. Also standing by to testify for the accused were low-level radiation expert Dr. Robert Woollard of the University of British Columbia and New Democrat MP Jim Manly, who had previously tabled a private member's bill (rejected by government) calling for a federal government enquiry into CFMETR.

But after twenty minutes of Crown witness

testimony, the judge declared he wouldn't allow any cross-examination intended to establish CFMETR as a threat to life, liberty and security of the person. The court was only concerned with the act of trespassing, not the motivation behind it, Judge Edward O'Donnell interjected when Tim began laying the groundwork for his clients' defence. The Charter of Rights and international law would have to wait for another day and another case.

It wasn't looking good for the eight women. If convicted, each faced a maximum possible penalty of $1,000 or twelve months in jail. However, the accused were ultimately vindicated by the tide tables, which the Crown and the DND had neglected to check before prosecuting. It turned out that the plucky picnickers never made it above the high-water line so no trespass was committed. Case dismissed.

"Did the military know they didn't have a case against us?" Liberty asked afterwards. "If so, why didn't they drop the charges? And if not, this makes one wonder what other important questions they don't have answers to—like what happens in the event of an accident aboard a nuclear submarine at Nanoose?"

The women considered their acquittal a dubious victory. "Though we were happy to be acquitted, we were disappointed that the evidence we had so carefully prepared would not be heard and that none of our expert witnesses was able to speak," they told their supporters.

At least one of those witnesses concurred. When I caught up with Bob Aldridge outside the courtroom and asked him what he thought of the outcome, he told me "It's nice to get an acquittal, but in a way I see it as part of the cover-up to not get the issues out. Canada has now joined the US in the judicial complicity cover-up of our war preparations and of the nature of the weapons we're designing."

Seventeen months and many arrests later, another NCCer finally made it before the bench. Brian Mills had been arrested along with eighteen other people for blockading the entrance to CFMETR on October 26, 1987—the twenty-fifth anniversary of the Cuban missile crisis. Fearing a media spectacle, the publicity-shy Crown subsequently dropped charges against all but Brian. When Brian finally did get his day, it stretched into two (spread over five months). But once again the NCC was unable to introduce the meatier legal arguments, and Brian was ultimately acquitted on a technicality. This time the Crown forgot to establish that the obstructed property was worth more than $1,000—a requirement for conviction on a charge of mischief involving property.

After the trial, Brian told me he was "pleasantly surprised" by the acquittal, which came on his thirty-eighth birthday. But, like the Motherpeace Eight, he was also disappointed. "I'd hoped to be able to open up the justice system to dealing with the larger issues at stake here," he said on the courthouse steps where he and two dozen supporters carved up a large birthday cake for a post-trial celebration. "It's time that the legality of preparation for nuclear war and the risk of environmental disaster posed by a nuclear accident were tested in a court of law."

Tim Leadem, who defended Brian, wasn't about to scoff at any acquittal. However, he agreed that the real victory would come when a case like this

was won using the Charter of Rights or international law. "It would be precedent setting certainly
in British Columbia and perhaps with ramifications
for peace groups throughout Canada if they eventually were acquitted on the substantive basis rather
than on any technical basis," he told me.

III. Grannies Go Gaga

For all their civilly disobedient efforts, the members of the NCC have never managed to serve up
their defence or to get anyone other than Brian and
the Motherpeace Eight in front of a judge. And the
NCC has not been alone in its quest to put the US
Navy's nuclear colony at Nanoose on trial.

More than once, Greenpeace has joined the
NCC in body and boat for water sports with
the Navy out on the range. On one jaunt, the
Nanoose peace navy's coalition forces were further augmented by a squadron of sprightly, silver-
haired crooners called the Raging Grannies. The
Grannies, with chapters now sprouting up across
Canada, are best known for their colourful shawls,
plastic-flowered bonnets and politicized verses to
favourite old-time tunes. The eccentric choir got its
start in Victoria in February 1987 when a group of
eight women (including two World War Two
veterans) decided they'd had enough of nuclear-
powered, nuclear-capable warships in their waters.
Today, Raging Grannies are a common sight (and
sound) at peace and environmental demonstrations
throughout BC's nuclear triangle. They've been fea-
tured on CBC's *Morningside* with Peter Gzowski
and *The National* with Knowlton Nash. As to their
effectiveness, the Grannies are so formidable that
in December 1990, the organizers of Victoria's First

Night celebration reportedly offered to pay the Victoria Grannies $200 if they would stay away from the city's New Year's festivities. The Grannies declined the cash.

On the peace front, two years after the Motherpeace Eight invaded what was almost DND's turf, Grandmother Peace set sail for Winchelsea Island in August 1988. And this time there would be no uncertainty about where they stood—and sang—in relation to the high tide line. When the Greenpeace ketch *Vega* deposited six Raging Grannies on the Winchelsea dock, they were immediately arrested. While the police attended to the paperwork, the spunky sextet broke into song:

> What shall we do with the base at Nanoose?
> Loaded with subs we wish would vamoose
> Give 'em a bunch of verbal abuse
> Early in the morning!"

After collecting their arrest notices, the vocal ensemble presented base officials with a submarine on rye, complete with an aluminum foil hull and conning tower, then shoved off.

"Faced with the choice of imprisoning hundreds of these grandmothers or following its own stated policy of being a nuclear-free country, what will the Canadian government and its people choose to do?" the NCC asked in its newsletter the following month. The government responded by displaying its usual aptitude for dodging tough choices. All charges were dropped. Apparently the prospect of stuffing little old ladies in jail cells unnerved our guardians of justice.

A sweeping legal precedent could be set if the NCC or any of its cohorts ever does get to use the campaign's carefully prepared defence. If Nanoose protesters were vindicated on the basis of the Canadian Charter of Rights or international law, the ruling could affect not only Nanoose, but other military hot spots in Canada, such as the cruise missile tests over northern Alberta and NATO low-level flights over Labrador. The precedent could even extend to peace activists in the US, since that country is also obliged (theoretically, at least) to respect international law. In addition, a full-length trial and subsequent appeals arising from a Nanoose protest would sharply focus public attention for months and possibly years on a relatively obscure aspect of US military activity in Canada. Within the defence ministry, such opportunities for glasnost are about as popular as an economic recession.

The notion of judicial complicity in a military cover-up may seem far-fetched. But it is certainly true that judges, in their refusal to hear legal arguments based on the Charter of Rights and international law, have insulated the status quo from public and legal scrutiny, even though the status quo is quite possibly illegal. Because of these court-room obstacles, and because of the Nanoose Conversion Campaign's overriding commitment to constructive, positive action, the NCC is not putting all of its strategy eggs in the civil disobedience basket.

Chapter 7

MAKING PEACE IN OUR OWN BACKYARD

*They say that the base brings
    employment
But conversion would give us much
    more
We'd like those jobs to be peaceful
So there'll be a future in store.*

Raging Grannies
(Tune: "My Bonnie Lies Over the Ocean")

Conversion. Since the NCC's debut in 1984, this has been the campaign's ultimate yet most elusive goal. And beyond the boundaries of the Navy's nuclear bay at Nanoose, the call for nationwide and worldwide conversion is moving into the spotlight for the peace and labour movements and even some governments. But what's in the word?

The Canadian Union of Public Employees, Canada's largest union, defines economic conversion as "the process through which workers, businesses, communities and nations move from a military to a civilian economy... At the central level, it involves political decisions to divert tax dollars from the military to serve human needs. Locally, it involves the planning and management needed to switch industries and plants over to the production of useful, marketable, civilian goods.''

Nanoose, of course, is a weapons testing facility, not an assembly line. So CUPE's definition of conversion needs to be expanded to include military bases as well as manufacturing plants. In the context of Nanoose, conversion refers to transforming the existing military facilities and natural resources of Nanoose Bay to nonmilitary, environmentally sound uses that will benefit the regional population. The NCC has always maintained that, in order to be successful, this local conversion must satisfy the needs of Canadian workers (civilian, not military) who now make their livelihood from the base, and it should not create a net loss of revenue to the regional economy. "The conversion process changes military facilities and industries to socially useful and productive facilities—providing secure jobs without contributing to global insecurity,'' the NCC states.

At the 1986 People's Enquiry into CFMETR, the conversion campaign members told the 500 participants that an "ideal" conversion of Nanoose would:

1. employ at least as many people as are presently employed at CFMETR;
2. employ all of the present civilian staff who choose to stay, with a minimum amount of retraining necessary;
3. provide a good quality of work environment for the employees;
4. fill a community or regional need that is not presently being met (the community or region must define its own needs);

5. encourage the growth of new industries in the region;
6. be environmentally sound and use local resources wisely;
7. be chosen by the local community and be in harmony with local community values;
8. be Canadian owned and operated using local and domestic suppliers of materials, equipment and components;
9. make efficient use of the existing buildings, grounds, equipment, materials and technology.

I. Welcome to Ground Zero

Although employee numbers vary somewhat from month to month, approximately 108 Canadians and 67 Americans draw a paycheque (from their respective governments) for their toil at CFMETR. Among the Canadians, 70 are permanent civilian staff, 15 are permanent military staff and 18 are commissionaires and temporary civilian and military staff. Only 4 Americans are permanent military staff at CFMETR, but temporary US military staff on site varies from 35 to 50. The US also keeps between 10 and 20 temporary civilian staff at the base.

According to the DND, CFMETR pumps $10 million into the regional economy each year. The NCC disputes the figure and reminds the public that "the danger to the local population and to nature's ecological balance from a nuclear accident on the Nanoose ranges is everpresent and would be an extreme price to pay for what may well be a negligible economic benefit."

The regional economy is not primarily dependent on the base—certainly not to the extent that other regional economies are tied to their bases, such as CFB Summerside in PEI, scheduled to close in 1992. In fact, the economy of all parts of Vancouver Island is closely tied to the region's abundant natural resources. Forestry, fishing and tourism are the economic mainstays, which is all the more reason to confiscate the US Navy's nuclear charge card at Nanoose Bay, the NCC says.

NCC supporters like Dr. Martin Spencer, a member of Canadian Physicians for the Prevention of Nuclear War, consider the personal and environmental risks posed by CFMETR to be so great that conversion is the only sane alternative. "In addition to fuelling the arms race, we who acquiesce to the activities at CFMETR are putting ourselves at risk in other ways," writes Spencer in the *Lantzville Log*, the newspaper serving the small community a few short kilometres from the Navy's nuclear warships and ASW tests. "In the event of nuclear war, those of us near Nanoose are living at Ground Zero. There is no question but that we are a prime military target. We are also placing our environment at risk at peacetime. . . We are all willing to take risks if the potential gain is sufficient. As a physician I make such decisions constantly. Here the product itself is not only harmful, it is the single most important public health issue facing mankind, for which prevention is the only treatment. There are peaceful and more productive uses for Nanoose. Let's start examining them."

II. Take Your Peaceful Job and Shove It

One group that's been staunchly (and predictably) opposed to the NCC's drive to send the US Navy packing and to demilitarize local waters is, ironically, the group the campaign would most like to bring on side: Local 1017 of the Union of National Defence Employees at CFMETR. While base officials smile and shake their heads when asked about the likelihood of the NCC ever retooling the base to anything other than a weapons testing station, the civilian employees are less carefree about the doings at the peace house across the bay.

"What those people are trying to do would eliminate my job," my mother's neighbour told me one day when the topic of our conversation wandered into the danger zone of my book. Doug is a civilian employee working at CFMETR's command centre on Winchelsea Island. There's not much overlap in our political perspectives, but Doug is as friendly as neighbours come. All he had to do was hear an ailing lawn mower or see a wobbly picnic table in my mother's yard, and he'd pop over with his tool box. In fact, the picnic table was responsible for our risky discussion of the NCC that day. I was giving the recently repaired table its annual paint job when Doug, who'd developed a proprietary attachment to the thing since bolting down a few loose boards, came over to inspect my work.

"You know, Doug," I replied, "they're not trying to close the base—they're trying to convert it. There could be just as many jobs, if not more."

"Are you kidding? If the government shuts us down, that's it. No more jobs. They're not going to worry about converting the place or finding us new jobs. And that's my bread and butter we're talking about."

John Kraeker, former president of UNDE Local 1017, shares Doug's worry. "Our major concern is jobs," Kraeker told the Nanaimo *Daily Free Press*.

"There are a lot of family people involved—it's a great concern. There's always the fear that if pressure groups create enough noise, politicians eventually react."

Yet, when you scratch a little deeper it turns out that Kraeker's real beef with the NCC is not just jobs, but what kind of jobs. The proposal to retrain and re-employ the current workers in new, nonmilitary jobs with comparable salaries is about as popular within Local 1017 as a complimentary subscription to *Peace Magazine*. The real issue from Kraeker's viewpoint isn't whether the workers could make out satisfactorily under conversion; it's why they should have to change jobs when they're happy with and proud of their current work.

"Another thing that sticks in our craw is that the conversion campaign wants us to become fish farmers, oyster shuckers and boatbuilders," Kraeker says. "But nobody ever asked us. We take a lot of pride in what we do. We have a very strong sense of unit identification and we're proud to be working for CFMETR... We've had a label hung on us as warmongers, but we like to see ourselves as protecting peace. We are all patriots."

Within the surrounding communities, the NCC's critics scoff at the group's intentions and dismiss the call for conversion as nothing more than a pipedream conjured up by a merry band of blissed-out peaceniks. "The [NCC's] ongoing attempt to frighten people into demanding the closing of our defence base and converting it into 'peaceful' activities (making bead necklaces and seashell brooches?) is well known," writes Canadian war veteran Bill English in a letter published in the Nanaimo *Times*.

III. Wooing the Public and the Workers

The NCC's vision for a converted Nanoose includes considerably more than hippie paraphernalia and tourist trinkets. The group hesitates to map out a specific proposal or conversion project for the site because campaign members believe all sectors of the community and region should collectively develop the best conversion plan for Nanoose. But to get the ball rolling, NCC members have floated various ideas about what direction the conversion could take. Among the suggestions are: a marine biology station for researching oil spills, marine ecology, water desalination, waste management or shellfish toxicology; a research and development (R&D) centre for alternative energies (wind power, tidal power and forest biomass being logical candidates within the region); an R&D centre for biotechnology or advanced industrial materials (two rapidly developing fields in which Canada has fallen far behind other industrial nations); a retirement village; a fertilizer production plant; a recycling centre; or an expansion of the mariculture industry already started in the bay. A converted Nanoose needn't be limited to any one proposal, the campaigners point out. A variety of enterprises could co-exist on the site. In fact, multiple-use would likely benefit the region more than single-use.

At the People's Enquiry, the NCC issued a public challenge to the communities surrounding Nanoose: "Let's get together now and start planning for conversion. With so many resources at hand . . . the area could develop innovative projects that would provide long-term income, job security, social benefits, and a good quality of life for many people in the local community. Or the local people can go on as they are now, hosting a military base that produces nothing, employs few, prevents alternative land use, costs all of us tax dollars, and may—at any time—be closed or cut back by government decisions over which we have little or no control." The NCC has always been quick to remind the public that the US government could pull the plug on CFMETR whenever the facility outlives its usefulness to the Navy. Canada would be left with little more than empty buildings since the US Navy owns the computers and underwater testing equipment used for the anti-submarine warfare research.

Nobody rose to the challenge, so the NCC later began soliciting support for a Community Alternate Uses Committee. Conversion campaigners hoped the committee would bring together local business, labour, government, public institutions and citizen groups to discuss alternative uses for CFMETR, to research their feasibility, and to map out a plan for conversion. The Nanaimo, Duncan and District Labour Council gave its formal endorsement to the concept. But no actual committee with community representation has ever met or even formed, due mainly to a lack of interest outside of the NCC.

As for Kraeker's assertion that no one ever asked the workers if they'd like to trade in their oscilloscopes for oyster knives, the conversion campaign says it's a bum rap. "The NCC has tried to talk with UNDE on at least three occasions, and I've personally tried to talk to John Kraeker," Laurie MacBride told me. "All we got was silence."

The base workers' resentment of the NCC was further fuelled during the campaign's three-year-long program of civil disobedience from 1985–1988. The conversionists threw up numerous blockades across the only road entrance to CFMETR, effectively barring workers from their job site (and paycheques). Not surprisingly, the workers perceived these blockades (which were often thoughtfully timed to coincide with shift changes) as unsolicited third-party picket lines.

Over the years, campaign members have grown increasingly concerned about winning the support of base workers. "The successful conversion of CFMETR to peaceful purposes will require the willing and enthusiastic participation of the workers, and they will require a great deal of support from the community," the NCC writes. In an attempt to build solidarity with the workers, the NCC agreed to a four-month moratorium on road blockades during a meeting with UNDE's regional representative at a BC Federation of Labour convention in December 1988. In exchange for the moratorium, the NCC hoped to finally get a face-to-face meeting with UNDE workers at Nanoose. The meeting never materialized. However, as of September 1991, the NCC had not resumed blockading the main entrance.

Ironically, despite the conversion campaign's numerous blockades, the only picket line violence that ever erupted at CFMETR involved a senior US civilian employee whose actions left a Canadian worker permanently disabled. When Roy Michaelis drove his four-wheel-drive truck through a legal Canadian picket line during the November 1989 nationwide strike by the Public Service Alliance of Canada (PSAC), he injured the picket captain, Brad Holmes. (UNDE is a component union of PSAC and was therefore involved in the strike.) While BCTV grabbed some visuals of the blood stains on the pavement, Brad was rushed to hospital with four crushed vertebrae and head wounds that took forty-six stitches to close. No charges were laid against Michaelis, and, after a brief hiatus, he returned to his post overseeing all technicians at the base's Winchelsea Island command centre. In an interesting endnote, Brad was one of more than 100 peace supporters who showed up on the steps of the Nanaimo cenotaph with candles in hand on the evening of January 15, 1991, the night before the United States began bombing Baghdad.

Despite this incident, the UNDE members still consider the peace house denizens across the bay a greater threat to their personal security than Uncle Sam. To cheer the gloomy pickets after Brad's injury, a couple of NCCers baked and hand-delivered a big platter of muffins to the picket line one morning. While treading the pavement later that day, John Kraeker told me the workers couldn't possibly accept the peaceniks' edible gift because "there's no telling what they put in them."

However, the NCC has persisted in its attempt to win a place in the workers' hearts. In 1990, campaign members drafted a policy statement supporting the right of defence workers to strike and to be granted conscientious objector status upon request: "NCC supports the right of defence workers to organize and take collective action for fair wages and benefits, job security, safety on the job, good working conditions, and a voice in determining how the product of their labour will be used. Further, NCC supports the right of defence workers to conscientious objector status in the workplace: i.e., workers who have moral or ethical reservations about any aspect of their work have the right to be reassigned to alternate jobs which are ethically acceptable to them with no resultant loss of wages, benefits, or job security.''

So far the members of UNDE Local 1017 appear to harbour reservations only about the Nanoose Conversion Campaign and not their own work at CFMETR. However, a quick survey of conversion efforts abroad shows that the NCC's goal of a converted, economically productive Nanoose is not as far-fetched as the nay-sayers believe.

Chapter 8

COURTING CONVERSION

What shall we do with all those sailors
Turn 'em into cooks and tailors
Farmers who will use hay balers
Early in the morning

Raging Grannies
(Tune: "Drunken Sailor")

Looking for that special holiday? That once in a lifetime experience? The one that will give you stories galore to share with the folks back home?

Treat yourself to old world charm and the latest in obsolete Warsaw Pact military might all at the same time. Stroll the historic streets of Krakow, sip Tokaji while overlooking the Wisla River at sunset, explore the magical Mazurian Lake district, then climb behind the controls of a MiG-21, buckle up and let 'er rip.

A mere $2,000 (US), plus a pilot's licence, puts you in the driver's seat of the Soviet-built fighter plane for one glorious, heart-pounding hour. (You're on your own for the other stuff.) No doubt the Polish defence ministry, whose future in the wake of a demilitarized Warsaw Pact was dubious at best, was only too glad to make itself useful to Poland's beleaguered economy. So some enterprising air force officers launched a company offering one-week holidays at Poland's military flying school at the Deblin airbase. A modest $500 covers your room and board for the week. However, getting war buffs airborne is where the government expects to rake in the hard currency. Although MiG-21s are predicted to be the aircraft of choice, guests can play Top Gun with a variety of Warsaw Pact hardware—all hired out by the Polish defence ministry.

Not to be outdone by some limp East bloc attempt at packaged fun, Israel grabbed the tourism spotlight shortly after the Gulf War by proudly announcing the country's newest joyride: Patriot Tours. If you've got the green, you too can see the launch sites from where the US Patriot missiles occasionally shot down those Saddam-sent Scuds.

Neither Poland's dollars-from-dogfights scheme nor Israel's Scud-buster outing offers a particularly admirable example of cashing in on a war gone bust. Israel's tourism gimmick doesn't qualify as even a primitive form of economic conversion. But both countries have, in their own crude way, stumbled upon conversion's fiscal fulcrum. Namely, that it's possible to turn a buck from a useless military artifact if you put your mind to it. In fact, despite the international peace movement's persistent, philosophically correct pleas for a nonviolent, demilitarized world, the conversion process is nearly always prompted by an economic rather than moral imperative.

I. Last One to Convert is a Rotten MiG

Shortly before Soviet economics, politics and nationhood dropped into their dizzying tailspin, the Soviet Union embarked on a dramatic program of economic conversion. It's anybody's guess where conversion will figure into the new scheme once the dust settles and we find out how many sovereign nations and national leaders occupy the geography once known as the Union of Soviet Socialist Republics. But it's a safe bet conversion will still be on the docket, because the country quite simply can no longer afford the war business. (The same can be said for all countries. But various social, political and economic factors cause some players in the armaments game to fold sooner than others.)

In December 1988, Soviet leader Mikhail Gorbachev delivered his first address to the United Nations. In it, he let the West know he wouldn't mind some friendly competition between superpowers in the conversion department. "We consider it desirable for all countries, especially the great military powers, to submit their national conversion plans to the United Nations," Gorbachev told the UN after announcing his country's intention to beat swords into pasta makers and baby strollers. He went on to urge all countries to support the creation of an international task force to evaluate the obstacles to conversion and report back to the UN.

To demonstrate his country's eagerness to get on with the job, Gorbachev declared that conversion of Soviet defence plants would begin the following year. A few months later, Western journalists got their first tour ever of a working Soviet defence plant producing advanced MiG-29 jet fighters—a plant slated for conversion. By 1992, the MiGs (or half of them, anyway) will disappear. In their place workers will be rivetting and glueing baby carriages, kids' toys, milk cartons and kitchen equipment. Apparently Soviet defence workers don't feel much cheerier toward conversion than John

Kraeker and the base workers at Nanoose. In the words of a Soviet arms factory employee: "I have been making missiles all my life. Now they want me to make saucepans!"

Nationwide, the Soviet plan called for cutting defence spending by 14.2 percent and military production by 19.5 percent by 1991. Food-processing equipment (canning machinery, chicken packagers, sausage makers, flour packers, juicers, milk pasteurizers and brewery equipment) figure high on Moscow's Most Wanted list. And no wonder in a country where crops and other foodstuffs routinely rot for lack of processing equipment. By the end of 1989, fifty-six factories, forty-five research and design establishments and 30,000 workers had regeared their output from munitions to farm-based food-processing equipment. Hi-tech home electronic gadgets (personal computers, VCRs, compact disc players and the like) are also on the conversion shopping list for Soviet consumers.

The reduction of military antagonism between the superpowers, which was kicked off in late 1987 with the signing of the Intermediate-range Nuclear Forces (INF) agreement removing short and medium-range Soviet and US land-based missiles from Europe, spurred the Soviet conversion program. Moscow was only too glad to patch things up with Washington after their forty-year spat so the sickly Soviet economy wouldn't need to lug a cancerous defence budget into the next decade. Gorbachev seized the opportunity to redirect dollars and announced various unilateral Soviet decisions to reduce troops and weaponry in Eastern Europe.

The INF agreement alone freed up the equivalent of $1 billion US for social spending in the Soviet Union. Milk pasteurizers and mobile refrigerators are already rolling off the Votkinsk factory assembly line that formerly produced the now-redundant missiles. In their conversion delirium, the Soviets are even trying to give the US a helping hand. Not surprisingly, the Soviet Union has set its foreign conversion sights first on America's Star Wars program—Ronald Reagan's Strategic Defence Initiative that's expected to soak the taxpayers for more than $160 billion and probably won't work, at that.

Why not convert the years of research and planning designed to put laser beam weapon systems in space into space-based solar power stations, the Soviets ask. The idea of space solar electric stations isn't new. But technical and financial obstacles have so far kept it in the land of science fiction. One of those obstacles is figuring out how to transmit energy from space—an obstacle the Star Wars beam weapon research could possibly solve. Another obstacle is the cost of placing energy-transmitting satellites in orbit. Andrei Gukov writing in *Soviet News and Views* suggests using the ground-based ballistic missiles eliminated by the INF agreement to launch the solar energy satellites into orbit. Alternatively, Soviet Air Force Major-General B. Surikov suggested the INF missiles headed for the scrap heap could be used to launch satellites for a space-based ecological monitoring program.

II. Star Spangled Switchovers

Countries with centralized, state-planned economies aren't the only ones able to summon a nationwide conversion campaign. In fact, the best historic example of a major, successful conversion program occurred in the United States. In the years following World War Two, military bases across the US closed down and in most cases were converted to civilian uses with assistance from the US Defence Department's Office of Economic Adjustment (OEA). In 1986, the OEA released a report documenting the effects of base closures and conversions in 100 communities during the previous twenty-five years. Although 93,424 civilian jobs were lost at the former US bases, the converted facilities ultimately supported 138,138 on-site jobs and 7,330 new off-site jobs—more than a 50 percent increase in civilian employment. (Unfortunately, the report doesn't say how many civilian defence workers laid off by base closures were re-employed in the new jobs created through conversion.) The OEA figures didn't include secondary employment (i.e., the extra jobs required to provide goods and services to the increased number of workers and their families), but that particular economic benefit may be balanced by the economic loss from the transfer of 136,823 military personnel resulting from the base closures.

Many of the former US bases are now airports, industrial complexes, colleges, technical training institutes, recreational facilities, municipal and regional health facilities and correctional sites. The Dauphin Island Air Force Station in Coden, Alabama, now houses the University of South Alabama's Marine Environmental Science Consortium. That conversion project spun twenty-six civilian jobs into sixty-six jobs through an effort that drew upon natural resources and existing facilities not unlike those at Nanoose Bay. And in Key West, Florida, the Truman Annex—a former military site—is now shared by Fort Taylor State Park, the Florida Marine Institute, several boatbuilding and sheet metal companies and the Monroe Mental Health Center.

Dozens of examples of similar "success" stories fill the pages of the OEA's reports and case studies.

Although the conversions were locally planned, a key component in their success was the federal government's support and commitment to the task. Conversion of any given site often took two to three years. The specific conversion plan for each site was designed primarily by the members of the affected community. The President's Economic Adjustment Committee chaired by the Secretary of Defense worked with local, state and federal agencies to help communities develop and carry out their conversion plans. Usually one or more levels of government contributed funds to stimulate private sector investments.

Despite America's impressive list of successful base conversions, the land of the free still boasts more than its share of the rocket's red glare. According to conversion guru Seymour Melman, author of *The Demilitarized Society* and numerous other books, the $8.2 trillion (US) spent on the US Defense Department budget during four decades of Cold War from 1949 to 1989 surpasses the entire monetary value of plant and equipment for US civilian industry in 1982 plus all the nation's infrastructure. "In other words," Melman writes in a 1991 article in *The Nation*, "the government has invested more capital in its military account than would be required to replace most of the human-made machines and structures in the country." The result of this investment is visible in America's mounting domestic crises of poverty, unemployment, inadequate health care, lack of affordable housing and the like. "When the nation's largest capital fund is used for products that lack use-value for consumption or further production, then decay of infrastructure and industry is to be expected,'' Melman continues. ''In the United States the burden of this plundering—a virtual war against our own people—falls most heavily on working people, minorities, children and all who have been made into a castoff population of homeless, hungry and untended sick.''

III. Pulling the Plug on Pinetree

Canada is not without its own examples of successful conversion, most notably the conversion of the CADIN/Pinetree radar stations spanning nine provinces. In 1985, Defence Minister Erik Nielsen announced that seventeen (later increased to eighteen) of the twenty-four stations would shut down. Four thousand jobs, half of them civilian, would be eliminated. The closure was a result of a US decision to withdraw its 49 percent funding of the stations, saying they had become obsolete—a decision over which Canada had no control, although Canadian communities would pay the price through unemployment. The Nanoose Conversion Campaign is quick to point out that a similar fate could await Nanoose.

One month after Nielsen's announcement, Ottawa put together an interdepartmental committee to oversee the closures and lessen the impact on the communities. With co-ordinated planning between the federal government, the Union of National Defence Employees and local impact committees, fifteen of the eighteen radar stations that closed between 1986 and 1988 have been (or are being) converted to civilian uses. Some of the new uses include: a retirement village, low-income housing, a skills training centre, a hail studies centre, a correctional facility, a native self-contained community, a school for problem children and an industrial park.

Of the three unconverted stations, one site was returned to its natural state at the request of the Alberta government (the facility was adjacent to a wildlife preserve). Another was transferred to the Kamloops Indian Board in BC. And the third, a remote radar site at Goose Bay, Labrador, will be torn down. "Due to its isolated location, there is no viable re-use for the site," Colonel Gerry Zypchen told me. Colonel Zypchen, a very helpful fellow who seems to be DND's most knowledgeable staff member on Canadian conversion activities, heads up Infrastructure Planning and Coordination for DND.

IV. Conversion Aversion

Less fortunate were the communities attached to the fourteen bases targetted for closure or downsizing in Finance Minister Michael Wilson's April 1989 budget announcement. Not surprisingly, the towns and provinces losing the 3,440 direct jobs to the base cutbacks got scared and angry. Few or no advance provisions had been made for retraining civilian employees or for refitting the facilities to alternative uses. Worse still, the affected communities had no prior warning of the economic bombshell until it was leaked the day prior to Wilson's budget speech. Defence Minister Bill McKnight later explained he couldn't consult with the affected communities in advance because the budget was confidential.

To appease the grumbling mayors and premiers, Ottawa offered its Industrial Adjustment Services

Program to set up local re-use committees that would bring base workers together with their affected communities for discussion and conversion planning. The communities were not impressed. "There will be no community left," a Summerside, PEI doctor lamented. "It will hurt everyone from home owners to bank managers."

In addition to Summerside, the thirteen other communities whose bases (or radar stations) got the chop were London, North Bay and Ottawa, Ont.; Winnipeg and Portage la Prairie, Man.; Sydney and Barrington, NS; Mont Apica, Que.; Holberg, BC; Gander, Nfld.; Moncton and Chatham, NB; and Penhold, Alta. On August 1, 1990, the radar stations at Sydney, Barrington, Holberg, Gander and Mont Apica closed. By the end of that same month, CFB Chatham's military airfield shut down. The remainder of the sites will "cease to exist" (as the DND folks say) or scale down between 1992 and 1996.

In terms of numbers, CFB Summerside was the hardest hit of the fourteen bases. The PEI community of 10,000 was expected to lose 1,300 direct jobs and 300 indirect jobs when the Armed Forces take a hike in spring of 1992. In the absence of conversion plans, civic leaders predicted one business in three might collapse. Portage La Prairie wasn't much better off, facing a potential loss of nearly 1,300 direct and indirect jobs in a city of 13,000.

Two weeks after Wilson broke the grim news, 10,000 PEI residents marched through downtown Summerside protesting the planned closure of their air base. A couple of months later, a union leader at CFB Portage La Prairie led a reportedly "raucous demonstration" temporarily blockading the entrance to the doomed base. The story repeated itself around the country wherever a base was slated for closure. Meanwhile, McKnight, who comes from a small town in Saskatchewan—the only province untouched by the base closures and reductions—said it "hurt" him to make the decision.

Local and provincial governments weren't the only ones steamed at the budget announcement. Liberal and New Democrat MPs began grilling McKnight in the House of Commons about the harshness of closing bases in economically needy areas with no prior plan for conversion. In fielding the flak, McKnight took a page from JFK's famous "Ask not what your country can do for you" entreaty and told his critics: "The men and women who serve in the military today . . . deserve the ability as Canadians to share the load in getting the debt down."

Although the Summerside closure represents the greatest loss of personnel at any single base, other communities around the country are bracing for (or already enduring) their own versions of economic crisis resulting from the scheduled closures. On the remote, northern tip of Vancouver Island, CFS Holberg (one of the few remaining radar stations from the old Pinetree line) lost virtually all of its 176 military personnel and 58 civilian staff in 1990. With family members added in, about 500 people were directly affected by the closure of Holberg. An additional 350 forestry workers and their families from a neighbouring forestry worksite who relied on the base's community services and facilities are also left in the lurch.

"Before it officially closed, Holberg accommodated approximately 500 people and had a 200 student-school, a 10-bed fully staffed hospital, curling rink, swimming pool, tennis courts, library, theatre, 120 apartments and 65 duplex sites," Nanoose Conversion Campaign supporter Deborah Ferens writes in the group's newsletter.

Silly and wasteful as it may sound, the government is apparently planning to plough under the Holberg complex (at a cost of $5 million to the taxpayer) rather than re-use it. (I guess that's one way to beat swords into ploughshares, although hardly the most desirable.) A local re-use committee was formed after the closure was announced, but the members threw in the towel a year later. At last report, only the school, still used by the children of the forestry camp, was to escape the bulldozers.

"I see that as a tremendous waste," Port Hardy Mayor Al Huddleston, a member of the short-lived Holberg re-use committee, told me. "It was a complete community. We wanted to see what opportunities there were for the base rather than just having it laid to waste." Huddleston, whose own community lost business revenue when CFS Holberg closed, was keen to see the Holberg complex converted to a community for seniors, the disabled or others in need of special services and a supportive social environment—a community for people who are unhappy with and poorly served by life in a large and impersonal city. Huddleston envisioned cottage industries, community programs designed by the residents, and economic savings on government programs currently serving victims of big city isolation. Although the innovative idea could have been a model for humane, forward-looking social planning, Huddleston found no takers for the proposal.

From the NCC's point of view, the recent spate of base closures lends strong support to the campaign's plea to get cracking on conversion planning for Nanoose rather than waiting until the US Navy decides the test range is obsolete and packs up its computers and goes home. "This situation [at Holberg] demonstrates clearly that a re-use committee needs to be established long before a base closes in order for the local community to find a successful alternative use," Ferens writes.

Dismal as the saga sounds for the fourteen bases and adjacent communities on Ottawa's budgetary hit list, many will probably undergo some form of economic conversion in the end. After all, the Pinetree conversions—a success story by most accounts—did not blossom overnight. So we shouldn't judge the outcome of this current round of closures on the basis of the initial panic attack gripping the affected communities.

However, if local re-use committees were at work right now in all base communities in the country, then those panic attacks and the crippling economic dislocations that can accompany unexpected base closures could be prevented or greatly reduced. As an added bonus, the conversion schemes devised for the eventual shutdown of bases would have the benefit of long-term planning rather than a desperate acceptance of whatever offers and investors happen to be handy during the crisis. The time has come for workers, communities and society to begin dealing with the conversion question actively rather than reactively.

At least four of the fourteen bases are on the road to conversion. Summerside will have a $20-million aerospace centre where its Tracker aircraft once frolicked. The centre, to be run by Slemon Park Corporation, is expected to create 300 jobs in the first four years and more down the road as additional tenants hang out their shingles. A community college has also been proposed for the site. As an added boost to the economically flattened community, the federal government plans to open a $38-million GST data processing centre (employing 400 people) in Summerside in 1992 to untangle the bureaucratic knot created by Michael Wilson's seven percent solution to the nation's deficit. And in April 1991, plans were unveiled for a multi-million-dollar Summerside resort designed to attract immigrant Hong Kong investors to Canada under the federal government's Immigrant Investor Project. (The resort and the GST centre are unrelated to the re-use of CFB Summerside and will not be located on the base.)

In Manitoba, Southport Aerospace Centre, Inc., is slated to take over the Portage La Prairie facility and provide privatized flight training for the Canadian Forces plus drum up aviation-related industry for the site after DND leaves in August 1992. The site will also house a technical training college to train people for jobs in the aerospace industry.

Elsewhere around the country, the Miramichi Airport Commission picked up the military airfield at Chatham and is now operating it as a civil airfield. The County of Cape Breton acquired the Sydney radar station, although the County's plans for the site aren't confirmed. Meanwhile, the municipality of Barrington took over the married quarters and related facilities at the Barrington radar station. The municipality intends to lease the housing and operate the rest of the complex as a community recreation site. The Mont Apica re-use committee, Colonel Zypchen tells me, is plugging away on conversion brainstorming but is somewhat stymied by the fact that the radar base is sitting in the middle of a provincial park. It's possible that Mont Apica, like Holberg, will be ploughed under in the end.

Government support has been a key element in these conversions. As Project Ploughshares researcher Ken Epps commented in assessing the Pinetree conversions: "Under conditions deemed strategically and politically appropriate by the government, Ottawa will actively participate in the replacement of military facilities by civilian ones, with minimized job loss." No matter what country you turn to in searching for examples of economic conversion of military bases or industries, one message comes through loud and clear: conversion projects that enjoy the support of the country's federal government work, and those that don't, don't.

Chapter 9

THE POLITICS OF
CONVERSION

There's no business like war business
The best business we know
Never mind the homeless and the
    hungry
Never mind the people without jobs
Nowhere can you get that special
    feeling
Like when you're piling up the bombs

Raging Grannies
(Tune: "There's No Business Like Show Business")

Every birdwatcher keeps a life list of all the species she has positively identified. Mine, I'm ashamed to admit, barely breaks 300, which is truly humiliating considering that it spans three continents. Nevertheless, I'm periodically able to tick off another "lifer" and nudge my tally up to a more respectable figure. However, the lifer I bagged while researching this book didn't go on my bird list, but my word list. (Wordwatchers keep life lists too.)

Fungibility.

Believe it or not, that was the word a flustered Joe Clark spat out in response to a ticklish question posed by Ed Broadbent about Canada's uranium exports. "This is an example of the application of the internationally accepted notion of fungibility," Clark told the New Democrat leader in 1985, while trying to dodge the ugly truth that Canadian uranium ends up in US nuclear warheads (many of which return to Canada aboard US warships at Nanoose Bay and elsewhere).

Contrary to Tory assurances that Canada—the world's largest producer and exporter of natural uranium—was only peddling its ore for peaceful uses (as required by the 1955 Canada–US nuclear cooperation agreement), Broadbent and a few thousand people in the peace movement had discovered that such quaint distinctions do not exist at US enrichment plants. Whether uranium is destined for a civilian reactor to light a US city or for a military reactor to breed plutonium for warheads, it all gets sent first to an enrichment plant where it's dumped in one big kettle. Broadbent felt Canada's External Affairs minister had some explaining to do.

"It is impossible to trace precisely each and every molecule of Canadian uranium through these complex enrichment plants," Clark huffily informed Broadbent. "However, for each ounce of Canadian uranium fed into the enrichment plant, the same amount, in both enriched and depleted forms as appropriate, is subject to the Canada–USA nuclear cooperation agreement and to the non-explosive and non-military use commitments contained therein."

In other words, no actual separation of uranium by country of origin or by intended use occurs. The "peaceful" status of Canadian uranium exists only in bookkeeping hyperspace. And that, says Clark, is an example of the application of the internationally accepted notion of fungibility (which in my dictionary translates to "interchange-ability").

I. From the Government that Brought You Free Trade

The verbal antics of Fungible Joe underscore the point that a society's ability to demilitarize and redirect its economic, technical and human resources away from industries of death and to-ward ones of social and ecological benefit is linked to government policies on a wide range of issues. Even if Brian Mulroney woke up in a cold sweat one night amid nightmares of nuclear holocaust at Na-noose, hopped out of bed and dashed off a note to George Bush cancelling the binational treaty gov-erning CFMETR, little would change for the rest of Canada. Economic conversion at a societal level will require substantial changes in numerous gov-ernment policies and practices.

For example, if the federal government declared Canada a nuclear weapons free zone and enforced that policy, US nuclear-armed warships would be prohibited from all Canadian ports including Nan-oose Bay—a move which would lend considerable momentum to the campaign to convert CFMETR. Similarly, if Canada were to withdraw from NATO, this would, among other things, substantially de-militarize Labrador whose Innu people now endure 7,000 over-flights per year of NATO aircraft. Gov-ernment policies regarding cruise missile testing, free trade, arms exports, uranium exports and de-fence spending further determine Canada's ability to move out of the pernicious ethos of militarism and get on with the legitimate and pressing needs of people and the environment.

Canada's three major political parties rate differently on this wide-ranging conversion scorecard. Starting with the party in power, despite Brian Mulroney's confession that enhancing the promise of peace is his "most cherished ambition," the Tories have been no pals of pax during their spin at the helm. In the summer of 1987, while the world awaited the two military superpowers signing a landmark disarmament agreement to remove and destroy intermediate-range nuclear missiles from Europe, Canada's defence minister released an astoundingly paranoid document. In his White Paper on defence, Perrin Beatty warned that Western Europe was at risk of being "subverted, overrun and destroyed" and vowed to protect Canada from the same fate with an $8-billion fleet of nuclear submarines and an array of other military mega-projects.

American military heavyweights scratched their heads and chuckled over Beatty's sub scheme, while General Alistair Mackie, a former British pilot, described it as "Canada's stick-on hairy chest." As history tells us, the subs never surfaced. But the Tories' truculence didn't die with the gutted White Paper.

Although media reports would lead one to believe the government is decreasing defence spending, in fact, the reverse is true. The $2.74 billion defence "cut" so widely touted in 1989 after Finance Minister Michael Wilson announced the base closures was in reality only a cut to the enormously bloated projections of the White Paper. Canada's 1989–90 defence budget of $11.34 billion was actually a $140 million increase over the previous year's budget. The 1990–91 defence budget came in around $12.3 billion after a supplementary $350 million was doled out to cover the Canadian Forces excursions to Oka, Quebec, and the Persian Gulf in 1990. And the country's 1991–92 defence budget soared to $13.2 billion.

Ironically, two months after the Persian Gulf war ended, recently installed Defence Minister Marcel Masse announced the cancellation of several weapons purchases and the elimination of 1,000 jobs at DND headquarters in Ottawa. As well, Masse put base-dependent communities on notice, saying that military bases exist to serve the Armed Forces and not vice versa. By June 1991, rumours of another round of Canadian base closures were thicker than the Monday morning crowd at a UI office. The next month, in a bid to curb Western disaffection with Ottawa, the federal government announced that none of Western Canada's thirteen military bases would be closed.

The search for Tory policies and decisions influencing the conversion process eventually brings one to the Canada–US Free Trade Act signed into law January 1989. Among its many modifications to Canada's economy, this agreement terminates all federal government subsidies to regional industrial development in Canada excluding the defence and oil industries for reasons of "national security." Such an arrangement can only stimulate defence production (particularly in economically depressed regions of the country) as various corporations move into or increase production of the only goods eligible for subsidies. It's not surprising that the US would tolerate Canada's defence industry exclusion since 50 to 80 percent of the military chattel produced in Canada is sold to the US.

Also thwarting conversion is Mulroney's warm

welcome (first approved under a Liberal administration) of US cruise missiles zipping over Canada
during the first three months of every year. Not
only does cruise testing once again cast Canada in
the role of helping the United States perfect its first
strike capability, the testing supports the continued
production of cruise missile components at Litton
Systems in Rexdale, Ontario. And as an added bonus,
Canada even gets to share liability (from 25 to 100
percent) for any crack-ups or other blunders resulting from the cruise tests in this country.

The Tory government continued its Cold War
posturing even after the cataclysmic changes in the
Soviet Union and Eastern Europe were well under
way. In justifying the $12 billion 1990–91 defence
budget, former Defence Minister Bill McKnight as-
serted, "The most serious direct threat to Canada is
a Soviet nuclear attack on North America." Yet the
1989 public opinion survey conducted by the Canadian Institute for International Peace and Security revealed that a scant 6 percent of the Canadian
public considered military threats the most serious
danger to Canadian security. Forty-three percent
said economic threats were the most serious, and
51 percent pegged environmental threats in the
number one spot.

By 1990, even the United States realized the
Cold War was history. "Nobody seriously believes
today that the Warsaw Pact any longer constitutes
a military threat to the West," US Defense Secretary
Dick Cheney acknowledged in September, seven
months before the Soviet-led military alliance disappeared altogether. Nevertheless, in the 1991–92
fiscal year, Ottawa is doling out $13.2 billion in
public funds to the military and a mere $1 billion to
the Department of the Environment (not counting

the much ballyhooed Green Plan which gets a skimpy $3 billion over a five-year period.)

One week after the April 1, 1991, disintegration of the thirty-six-year-old Warsaw Pact, Canada's External Affairs minister proved once again that he could boldly go where no logic or moral decency had gone before. On the subject of Canada's role in disarmament and arms control, Joe Clark stated that "Our intention is to not launch an initiative into these waters." (If only he felt the same about the ASW weapons launched at Nanoose.) "We do not believe there would be merit in premature action that has little chance of moving the process forward," Clark told the North Pacific Cooperative Security Dialogue conference. "Nor do I view my own country as the one to take a lead in this area." (Barbara McDougall has since replaced Clark on the External Affairs portfolio, thereby demonstrating the fungibility of Tory cabinet ministers.)

As for the Tory position on the prospect of converting CFMETR at Nanoose Bay, "DND does not plan to close or reduce the operations of [CFMETR] in the foreseeable future," Bill McKnight told me flatly before he was shunted off to the agriculture portfolio. "The Nanoose military facility will therefore continue operations in accordance with existing bilateral agreements between Canada and the United States."

II. Liberal Latitudes

The Liberals' record for deal-making and cobbling together policies based on political expediency does not inspire hope that this will be the party to systematically redirect military resources to civilian needs. At present, the Liberals are operating in a policy vacuum where defence (among other things) is concerned. Even though the Liberals form the official opposition in Canada, they haven't managed to put pen to paper and draft a comprehensive defence policy, unlike their two political rivals. Instead, the Liberals limit themselves to bashing specific Tory activities when it's politically advantageous—even when those same activities were originally approved by their own party.

The cruise missile testing is the classic example of the Liberal party's moral and political flexibility. Although the Liberals now claim to oppose cruise missile testing over Canada, the Canada–US Test and Evaluation Program permitting the testing was signed in February 1983, when Pierre Trudeau was prime minister. According to the rumour mill, anti-nuke Trudeau got himself into the political pickle by agreeing to swap cruise tests for no duty on softwood lumber. The story has never been verified, and probably never will be, though a Pentagon official who specializes in NATO negotiations says the US regularly trades economic concessions for military ones. "It's the way of the world," the unnamed source was quoted as saying in a 1988 article by Vancouver *Sun* columnist Jamie Lamb. "Nobody talks about it much, but most of our allies come to us in need of some economic relief or advantage and, lacking anything in the way of economic levers themselves, often find that they can get what they want by making military agreements. It happens regularly. Canada's no exception."

Nor does the Liberal party's integrity index soar on other military matters. One week before the international arms bazaar, ARMX-89, was held in Ottawa, Liberal External Affairs critic André Ouellet rose in the House and trashed the Tory government's involvement in the event sponsored biannually by Toronto's Baxter Publishing, which puts out *Canadian Defence Quarterly*. With righteous indignation, Ouellet announced that Liberals will not tolerate "this profitable and scandalous effort to sell weapons to Third World countries." Ouellet was reminded by Associate Defence Minister Mary Collins that ARMX debuted in 1983 with the approval of the Trudeau government. In the same debate, New Democrat MP Dan Heap pointed out that "the last Liberal government. . . approved the sale of spare parts for tanks to the Chilean government headed by the dictator [Augusto] Pinochet."

On the subject of economic conversion for Nanoose and more generally for Canada, the Liberal position is noncommittal. When I asked Ouellet whether his party supported the NCC's goal to convert Nanoose, I received an answer that left all options open. "Any decision to change existing defence co-operation arrangements with Canada's NATO allies must be based on a clear-cut rationale justifying the change," Ouellet told me. (Like the Tories, the Liberals shudder at the thought of pulling Canada out of NATO.) "The Liberal Party would use two main criteria," Ouellet continued. "Whether the activity was consistent with Canada's international security goals, and the state of international negotiations to reduce the level of military confrontation."

Hmmm, I thought. Okay. Well how about economic conversion more generally in Canada?

"The Liberal Party supports *in principle* the concept of economic conversion," Ouellet wrote (his emphasis). But to save his party from having to rush right out and draft a conversion program, he added "many factors must be taken into account before a national government can determine how to proceed with a program of conversion."

III. Halfway There with the NDP

The New Democratic Party's defence policies are the most conducive to economic conversion. However, they aren't everything a disarmer might desire. The NDP policy is firmly anti-nuclear and would rid Canada of all nuclear weapons and their components. The NDP plan would also see Canada pull out of the NATO alliance, terminate the NORAD agreement with the United States and adopt an independent defence policy. But since voters haven't yet seen fit to give the federal NDP the opportunity to put its policies where its mouth is, all disarmers can do at this point is take the party at its word.

In keeping with the NDP's overall plan to detach Canada from all military alliances with the United States, the party objects to the US military presence at CFMETR. At its 1985 federal convention, the party passed an emergency resolution opposing the impending 1986 treaty renewal of the binational agreement governing the use of CFMETR. The NDP also opposes the presence of nuclear weapons aboard US vessels at Nanoose and other Canadian harbours. In December 1985, New Democrat MP Jim Manly from Vancouver Island introduced a private member's bill in the House of Commons demanding that the federal government conduct a public enquiry into CFMETR before the 1986 treaty renewal. The bill died when its allotted discussion time was talked out by Nanaimo's Tory MP Ted Schellenberg, who launched into a lengthy and largely irrelevant oration on the natural and human history of Nanoose Bay.

However, the NDP's defence policy does not support conversion of conventional weapons production or deployment. In fact, NDP policy directly contradicts conversion of Canada's non-nuclear military industries and bases. The NDP policy calls for building an independent Canadian military industrial base and independent armed forces—two tasks now shared with the United States. A shift to nonalliance needn't increase militarization in Canada. On the contrary, disengaging from the United States' global military strategies would appear to be an essential step along the path to economic conversion. Unfortunately, the NDP formula for Canadian military independence would invigorate non-nuclear domestic defence production and increase the need (and the budget) for Canadian military facilities and personnel.

As for economic conversion at Nanoose Bay or, more generally, for Canada, NDP Defence Critic Derek Blackburn told me in 1989 that his party's policies for economic conversion "are still being developed." (My more recent queries to the party on this topic were not answered.) In September 1989, NDP MP Dan Heap tabled a private member's bill calling for conversion but only of defence plants filling nuclear weapons contracts.

It's not surprising that the party of labour is dragging its feet on drafting a comprehensive conversion policy. Organized labour itself has had a tough time getting all its members under one roof on the subject of economic conversion. However, no matter which party is in power, top-down changes to federal government policy are only one part of the conversion story. A grassroots movement that fosters widespread popular support for conversion and that unites union members with conversion advocates and the peace movement is equally essential.

Chapter 10

WE AIN'T GONNA STUDY WAR NO MORE

Now this story's ending sadly, it is true
But guess who can rewrite it—me and
  you!
I think we always knew it
We don't have to let them do it
And they'll get used to peacetime
  when it comes

Raging Grannies
(Tune: "She'll Be Coming 'Round the Mountain")

Although you wouldn't know it from the Nanoose base workers' scorn of the proposal to convert CFMETR, those who earn their living from military enterprises aren't always so resistant to conversion. In fact, one of the most remarkable examples of the potential for worker-driven conversion was the dream of the employees at Lucas Aerospace—Britain's largest private military contractor.

When Lucas management sacked 5,000 employees between 1970 and 1974 and threatened that thousands more would follow, the remaining 13,000 workers responded by drafting a detailed plan for converting the seventeen Lucas plants to non-military production. In their 1,200-page Alternative Corporate Plan, they proposed 150 socially useful products the company could produce with the existing equipment and employees, ranging from solar heating components and wind generators to agricultural equipment and aids for the disabled. The workers augmented their pitch to Lucas execs by churning out an array of product prototypes. Management yawned. Lucas's biggest customer, Britain's Labour government, wasn't much perkier.

In 1978, the Lucas Aerospace Combine Shop Stewards Committee, which organized the Plan, was nominated for a Nobel Peace Prize. Three years later, Lucas fired Combine leader Mike Cooley. "Rather than just talking about the politics of conversion, we wanted to show politicians, scientists and engineers what was possible," Cooley later said. "We did not believe that it was in the national interest that all that science and technology should be wasted."

I. Labouring for Conversion

Even though the Lucas employees' ambitious Corporate Plan never made it off the drawing board, it has inspired conversion campaigns elsewhere and remains an internationally renowned example of workers' ability to develop economically, socially and environmentally sound alternatives to military production.

In Canada, the lack of satisfactory advance planning, research or discussion about economic conversion has contributed to the adversarial relationship between defence workers and the peace movement. And the rest of the labour movement is very sensitive to the fact that disarmament and demilitarization without orderly conversion will result in job losses. "Part of the reason the arms race continues to escalate is that people fear the economic effects of disarmament," the Canadian Union of Public Employees (CUPE) stated in its bimonthly journal, *The Facts*. "After all, no one wants to lose his or her job because a factory making military components closes. The essence of economic conversion is orderly planning so people won't be hurt by the switch to a peacetime economy. Working for disarmament without planning conversion may be futile."

The labour movement both nationally and internationally is adding its voice (if somewhat sporadically) to the call for economic conversion, and not only because conversion will save defence employees from the UI line. It's no secret that military spending is directly linked to unemployment in other sectors. Two and half times as many jobs can be created in education as in defence for the same amount of government dollars. Health care, construction and mass transit also peg in well ahead of the military on a jobs-per-dollar basis, according to the US Bureau of Statistics. When a society is saddled with structural unemployment, statistics like these become very relevant.

In 1989, the Ontario Federation of Labour braved the wrath of base and defence industry workers and sponsored a conference examining the prospects for and implications of economic conversion of Canada's war plants and bases. And as far back as 1984, CUPE, which is Canada's largest union and the loudest labour voice calling for conversion, proposed five specific initiatives to stimulate conversion:

1. Require (through legislation) every major defence contractor to establish a conversion department to identify socially needed civilian applications of existing military technology and to conduct the necessary market research to determine the commercial viability of the projects.
2. Establish Alternative Use Committees in all major municipalities to identify local defence production facilities and to assist conversion planning. All relevant sectors of the community should be represented on the committee.
3. Create a National Conversion Council to sponsor and finance research projects on conversion. The Council should be funded with the money now spent subsidizing the export of weapons by defence industries.
4. Defence industry workers should negotiate conversion committees at their jobsites to determine how skills and technology in each company could best be put to alternative uses.
5. Reduce overall defence spending with a corresponding increase in funding for public and social services.

These initiatives, outlined by John Calvert in CUPE's journal, *The Facts*, could readily be expanded to include conversion of military bases. The workers and communities devastated by the recent round of Canadian base closures would surely be in better shape now if community alternative use committees and on-site conversion committees had been up and running before former Finance Minister Michael Wilson dropped his bombshell in April 1989. Such committees are precisely what the Nanoose Conversion Campaign has been lobbying for locally to retool the US Navy's nuclear outpost at Nanoose Bay into a benign facility.

II. UNDE the Volcano

The call to convert is not universally embraced by organized labour. The Union of National Defence Employees (UNDE), which is the largest of the eighteen component unions of the Public Service Alliance of Canada (PSAC), has repeatedly stymied attempts to ratify policies on conversion and other disarmament-related issues at various provincial and national labour conventions. In May 1989, one month after Finance Minister Michael Wilson announced the $2.74 billion of cuts to the defence budget, PSAC pledged it would spend $100,000 to fight the cuts.

Back in 1984 the BC Federation of Labour passed a resolution calling for Canadian withdrawal from NATO and a ban on nuclear-capable warships in Canadian ports. UNDE subsequently withdrew from nearly every provincial labour federation in the country as well as from the national Canadian Labour Congress, and it stayed out for three years. In defence of its walkout, UNDE said the BC Fed resolution, if adopted by government, would eliminate 5,000 civilian jobs at military sites. (UNDE's tangle with the pro-peace sentiments of the BC Fed was just one in a long string of standoffs between UNDE and the rest of organized labour throughout the early 1980s.)

"The Union of National Defence Employees has had to walk a fine line in the house of labour," UNDE's Ottawa headquarters informed me in 1991.

"It is no secret that the labour movement in Canada has always called for a reduction in National Defence's budget, which would mean a reduction in services provided by the civilian component in the Department, and therefore, ultimately, our members' jobs. While we support most of the labour movement's policies, this is one that, of course, we have always been at odds with."

UNDE rejoined the CLC in 1987 after the Congress adopted a position paper on national defence "which we could all live with," the folks at UNDE headquarters told me. The CLC document, billed as a "report to deal with clarification of PSAC/UNDE situation regarding CLC convention policies on peace, security and disarmament," must have been a disappointment to peace workers, not to mention the New Democratic Party. The position paper recommended Canada remain in NATO and lamented the "deplorable condition of Canada's armed forces"—a phrase which hardly paves the way for cuts to the defence budget. (On the bright side for peace workers, the CLC advocated NWFZ status for Canada and Canadian withdrawal from the NORAD agreement.)

The next year, with UNDE back in the fold, the CLC actually adopted a policy advocating economic conversion. Well, sort of. The ambiguous wording of the policy hints at the fierce resistance the CLC would have met had the Congress tried to pass anything stronger or more specific. "In our pursuit of immediate further disarmament steps we will, among other issues, actively promote . . . with the full participation and consultation of the trade unions involved, a major infusion of funds allocated by government for conversion research, followed by the implementation of orderly conversion of un-

necessary military production into civilian industries, ensuring that adequate measures are taken to
provide retraining and employment protection for
those affected,'' the CLC stated in its 1988 policy
document.

The policy makes no mention of converting
bases (which is where all UNDE workers are found),
just defence manufacturing plants. And by target-
ting only the vague entity of "unnecessary" military production for conversion, the CLC effectively
left the door open for workers at each and every
war plant in the country to insist that theirs is part
of the nation's necessary military production and
must therefore be exempt from conversion.

Canadian Auto Workers president Bob White,
whose members are among the nation's defence
industry workers, conceded that the CLC's six-page
peace policy (which dealt with much more than just
conversion and was titled ''Preparing for Peace—
Labour's Vision'') was indeed a ''consensus document'' designed to get all the major players in the
Canadian labour movement lined up on the same
side of the fence.

III. Going National

Within the Canadian peace movement, the Nanoose
Conversion Campaign and certain other conversion
advocates are pushing for a national conversion
effort. The NCC members, although sharply focussing
their work on the campaign's three-point agenda for
local conversion, have never limited their vision to
the narrow geographic boundaries of Nanoose Bay.
''With the involvement and united effort of community leaders, business people, labour unions, public
interest groups and all levels of government, the

successful conversion of CFMETR can be part of a broad campaign to effect economic conversion and revitalization within the Canadian economy," NCC member Laurie MacBride told the 1986 People's Enquiry.

Big dreams for a little group. But by June 1990, some of those dreams were translated into action (or at least the promise of action) when delegates at the Canadian Peace Alliance's annual convention endorsed a proposal put forward by the NCC and two other peace groups to embark on a national conversion campaign. The goals of the national campaign include slashing the defence budget, cancelling the Canada–US Defence Production Sharing Agreement and the Defence Industry Productivity Program, and making the federal government conduct a national conversion study to plan for converting some of Canada's defence plants. Oddly, the goals of the national campaign make no mention of converting bases despite the NCC's involvement in spurring this larger campaign.

The decision to underwrite a national conversion campaign put some teeth at long last into the CPA's original statement of purpose drafted at the alliance's founding convention five years earlier. One of the seven basic goals adopted by the fledgling CPA in November 1985 was "the redirection of funds from wasteful military spending to the funding of human needs through a program of conversion and retraining, promoting the development of a peace-oriented economy."

Today the CPA roll call includes more than 420 organizations, and the 2.2-million-member Canadian Labour Congress is among them. NCCers were understandably elated when they got a thumbs-up on their proposal for a national conversion campaign. But ironically, the Persian Gulf crisis, which flared up two months after the CPA's June 1990 convention, curtailed the CPA's involvement in the national conversion campaign while the Toronto-based alliance diverted its energies to opposing the war and simultaneously trying to get its national Citizens' Inquiry into Peace and Security off the ground. The newly formed Vancouver Island Conversion Committee, along with the Lethbridge Coalition for Nuclear Disarmament and Greenpeace/Defence Watch, found they had been left to carry the can on the national conversion campaign.

"Even as the peace movement brings its considerable energies to bear on stopping the Gulf War, we on the Vancouver Island Conversion Committee feel committed to keeping the national conversion campaign alive," VICC member Deborah Ferens wrote in *Disarming News* shortly after George Bush began levelling Baghdad with the help of Canada's CF-18s. "For in the long haul, the prevention of war and violence will depend a great deal upon building the foundation for and instituting the process of economic conversion." As of September 1991, VICC and the two other groups involved in the national conversion campaign were in a holding pattern, waiting to hear what money (if any) the financially anemic CPA would send their way to get things moving.

Despite the uncertain future of the CPA-endorsed national conversion campaign, the issue of redirecting military dollars and resources to socially and environmentally useful purposes is certain to draw increasing support and action in coming years. However, pulling the plug on the war machine will require an even deeper, more fundamental conversion—something Victoria's Bishop Remi De Roo calls "cultural" conversion.

"The kind of economic conversion for peace required in this country is not really possible without a transformation of societal values, ideals and priorities," Bishop De Roo told the Vancouver Centennial Peace and Disarmament Symposium in 1986. "We have ideologies deeply embedded in our culture and society which serve to rationalize a global war economy and Canada's role in it. . . What Canadians really need is a dynamic strategy of cultural education for peace: we need to unmask the dominant myths and discover the true meaning of peace."

The Nanoose Conversion Campaign is one small part of the cultural conversion process. For in their tiny blue-green corner of our blue-green planet, the members of the NCC are seeking far more than the conversion of a single weapons testing facility. In the words of Motherpeace veteran Sunshine Goldstream: "Being at peace is more than the absence of war. It means re-evaluating our jobs, our investments, our neighbours (far and near), our attitudes toward the environment—you name it. If we take our dedication to peace seriously, it affects everything we do, feel and think."

EPILOGUE

There is no way to peace, peace is the
way.

A.J. Muste

It often seems that the ethos of militarism is ines-
capable, permeating every mind, every action,
every aspect of social life. So what can we do? What
can anyone do?

This is the difficult question the Nanoose Conversion Campaign takes on day after day, year after
year, exposing a small but sturdy answer patiently
awaiting attention: We do what we can. Whatever
that is and for as long as it takes, which may be a
lifetime.

The NCC people have been acting on that knowledge all these years—while they were living in
tipis, holding winter solstice celebrations to welcome the return of the sun, lying on the pavement
at the base gates, dressing up like cleaning ladies to
sweep away nuclear radiation, and countless other
behavioural oddities that initially struck me as silly,
ineffective and more than a little flaky. These people were doing what they could.

The eight women who invaded Winchelsea Island in 1986 to reclaim it for peace three days
before Hiroshima Day were also doing what they
could. "A picnic is a symbolic act on several lev-

els,'' they wrote. ''Breaking bread together has traditionally been important for a community of people with a commitment to a common concern. Second, we are working for a world in which 'bread not bombs' is a reality for everyone. And third, it is our hope that ten years from now, with conversion of Nanoose to peaceful uses, we will be able to return for another picnic, bringing our children with us and not having to break any laws to do so.''

> You can forbid nearly everything
> But you can't forbid us to think
> And you can't forbid our tears to flow
> And you can't shut our mouths when we
>   sing.

Their words danced on the wind, racing the retreating surf along the rocky foreshore. The endless keening of gulls and the percussive hiss of the breaking waves insinuated themselves into the defiant chorus, creating a symphony of resistance that was whipped and buffeted across the sea. Although no one may have noticed, time briefly came to a halt while a single, suspended moment—a moment that was simultaneously very small yet immensely powerful—awaited its name. And in that moment, I discovered I had been following something much larger than an eight-inch newspaper story molded to fit the ''peaceniks clash with military'' formula. I had been witnessing the creation, or at least the sketchy blueprint, of an alternative reality—a reality so profoundly different from the one we know that it is virtually invisible to the uninitiated.

It's time Canada stopped hitchhiking its way through geo-politics, tossing in a few quarters for gas money while squeezed into the crowded back seat of America's macabre, runaway hearse. It's time Canada bailed out no matter what the speed and sought a road less travelled. A road whose miles are measured in a morality that places life above profits and power. A road sculpted by the courage required to find alternatives to war. A road whose journeyers seek justice for millions of people and for a planet suffocating beneath the monstrous burden of military expenditures. A road not *to* peace but *of* peace. A road that will lead, among its many destinations, to a nuclear-free and converted Nanoose.

West coast of North America, northern California to Alaska

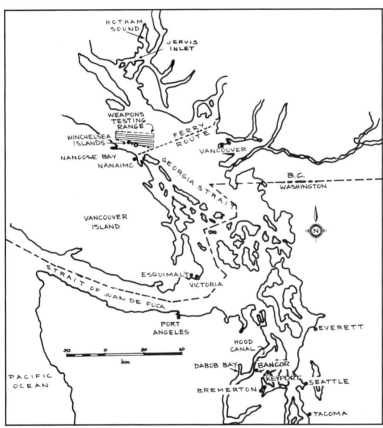

Vancouver, southern Vancouver Island, Puget Sound

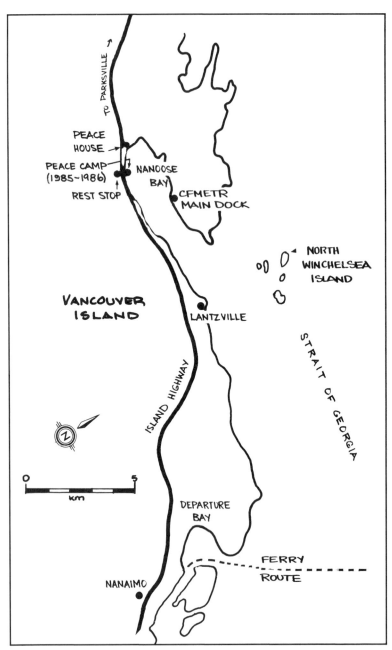

East coast of Vancouver Island from Nanaimo to Nanoose Bay

BIBLIOGRAPHY

Aldridge, Robert. *First Strike! The Pentagon's Strategy for Nuclear War*. Boston: South End, 1983.

Arkin, William, and Joshua Handler. *Neptune Papers No. 3. Naval Accidents 1945–1988*. Washington: Greenpeace, June 1989.

Calvert, John. "Military Conversion: Turning Arms Spending to Social Uses." *The Facts*, May 1984: 13–16.

Canada. *Challenge and Commitment: A Defence Policy for Canada*. Ottawa: Minister of Supply and Services, June 1987.

Canadian Union of Public Employees. "Economic Conversion." *The Facts*, March/April 1987: 6–8.

Davis, Jackson W. *Nuclear Accidents on Military Vessels in Canadian Ports: Site-Specific Analyses for Esquimalt/Victoria*. Victoria: Canadian Physicians for the Prevention of Nuclear War, October 1987.

De Roo, Bishop Remi. "Our War Economy and Conversion for Peace." *End the Arms Race: Fund Human Needs*. Vancouver: Gordon Soules, 1986.

Epps, Ken. "Closing the Pinetree Line." *Ploughshares Monitor*, March 1988: 16–17.

Garrett III, Lawrence H., and Admiral Frank B. Kelso, and General A.M. Gray. "The Way Ahead." *Proceedings*. U.S. Naval Institute, April 1991.

Gorbachev, Mikhail. "Address at the United Nations. New York, December 7, 1988." Moscow: Novosti Press Agency, 1988.

Handler, Joshua, and William Arkin. *Neptune Papers No. 2. Nuclear Warships and Naval Nuclear Weapons: A Complete Inventory*. Washington: Greenpeace, May 1988.

Handler, Joshua, and Amy Wickenheiser, and William Arkin. *Neptune Papers No. 4. Naval Safety 1989: The Year of the Accident*. Washington: Greenpeace, April 1990.

Handler, Joshua, and William Arkin. *Neptune Papers No. 5. Nuclear Warships and Naval Nuclear Weapons 1990: A Complete Inventory*. Washington: Greenpeace, September 1990.

Knelman, F.H. *America, God and the Bomb*. Vancouver: New Star, 1987.

Lamb, Jamie. "Was a Deal Made to Trade Lumber for US Missiles?" *Vancouver Sun*, March 11, 1988: B3.

Lawyers for Social Responsibility (Halifax). "The Porting of Nuclear Weapons-Capable Vessels in Canadian Harbours: A Policy Statement." Halifax: May 1987.

Melman, Seymour. "Military State Capitalism." *The Nation*, May 20, 1991.

Nanoose Conversion Campaign. "CFMETR and the Economics of Conversion." *Proceedings of People's Enquiry into CFMETR at Nanoose Bay, BC*. Gabriola: Gabriola Island Peace Association, 1986.

Raging Grannies. *The Raging Grannies Song–Cookbook: Volume I*. Gabriola: Gabriola Raging Grannies, 1989.

United States Office of Economic Adjustment. *1961–1986: 25 Years of Civilian Re-use. Summary of Completed Military Base Economic Adjustment Projects*. Washington: Department of Defense, April–May 1986.

United States Pacific Fleet, Commander Third Fleet. *United States Navy Instruction Manual.* Pearl Harbor: Department of Defense, May 1984.

Watkins, Admiral James D. "The Maritime Strategy." *Proceedings (Special Supplement).* US Naval Institute. January 1986.